19.95

Collectors' Information Bureau's

COLLECTIBLES

MARKET GUIDE & PRICE INDEX

Limited Edition: Plates • Figurines • Bells • Graphics • Ornaments • Dolls • Steins

Tenth Anniversary Edition

Collectors' Information Bureau
Grand Rapids, Michigan

Inquiries to the Collectors' Information Bureau
should be mailed to 2420 Burton S.E.,
Grand Rapids, Michigan 49546
Phone (616) 942-6898

Distributed by Wallace-Homestead,
a division of Chilton Book Company

Manufactured in the United States of America

Library of Congress Catalog Card Number: 83-61660

ISBN 0-930785-12-6 Collectors' Information Bureau

ISBN 0-87069-681-5 Wallace Homestead

1 2 3 4 5 6 7 8 9 0   9 8 7 6 5 4 3 2

CREDITS

Book Cover Design, Color Section Layout and Photo Styling:
Philip B. Schaafsma Photography, Grand Rapids, Michigan

Book Design and Graphics:
Trade Typographers, Inc., Grand Rapids, Michigan

1. "Bride & Groom" by Artaffects, Ltd.
2. "Time For Bed" from Enesco Memories of Yesterday Society
3. "1990 Betsy Ross" by Annalee Mobilitee Dolls, Inc.
4. "Father Christmas" by Lenox Collections
5. "Glorya" by The Constance Collection
6. The Night Before Christmas Collection by Goebel Miniatures
7. "Santa Entry/Fireplace" by Whitley Bay
8. "Springtime Gathering" by Hamilton Gifts, Ltd.
9. "We Are God's Workmanship" from Enesco Precious Moments Club
10. "Autumn Magic" by ANRI
11. "Feeding Time" by Royal Doulton
12. "Fifty Years of Oz" by The Hamilton Collection
13. "On the Threshold" by Woodmere China-copyright The Balliol Corporation
14. "A Child Is Born" by Reco International Corp.
15. "The Finishing Touch" by Flambro Imports

16. "Sitting Pretty" by The Norman Rockwell Gallery
17. "Crossroads" (Hum 331) Commemorative Edition by Goebel
18. British Traditions Books and Bookends-"The Printers" and "The Bookbinders" by John Hine Studios, Inc.
19. "Gurneyfoot and Shadra" by Precious Art/Panton
20. "Victoria Station" by Department 56, Inc.
21. "St. Peter's Cove" by Lilliput Lane Limited
22. "Tee Time at St. Andrew's" by Roman, Inc.
23. "Unexpected Rescuer" by LEGENDS
24. "Nicole" by Goebel, Inc.
25. "Aubrey" by Nahrgang Collection
26. "Cherie" by Gorham, Inc.
27. "Attack" by The Lance Corporation
28. "Delicate Motion" by Maruri U.S.A.
29. Carolers by Byers' Choice
30. "Argos" by Kaiser Porcelain USA, Inc.
31. "Medieval Santa" by Duncan Royale

Contents

About the Editors

Executive Editor
Diane Carnevale Jones

Diane Carnevale Jones is the principal of Professional Marketing Services, a Grand Rapids, Michigan based firm which specializes in media relations, market research and promotions for companies in the collectibles, gourmet cookware and manufacturing fields.

As an experienced collector herself, Ms. Carnevale Jones takes a special interest in the limited edition collectibles field and is very knowledgeable about the secondary market. Since September 1986, she has been Executive Director of the COLLECTORS' INFORMATION BUREAU. Prior to this, Ms. Carnevale Jones provided enthusiastic and innovative service to the BUREAU almost since its inception and was the Managing Editor for prior editions of this book.

Ms. Carnevale Jones researches and prepares secondary market columns for *Collector Editions* and *Collections* magazines and is a guest writer for other collectible publications. She also lectures and conducts seminars on a number of collectible topics.

Ms. Carnevale Jones holds a B.A. degree in English and journalism from the University of Michigan and resides in Grand Rapids with her husband and two children.

Managing Editor
Cindy Zagumny

Cindy Zagumny is the Executive Administrator and Managing Editor of the *Collectibles Market Guide & Price Index*. She graduated from Michigan State University with a Bachelor of Science Degree in retailing and business from the College of Human Ecology.

Ms. Zagumny previously worked in the retail, medical and insurance fields for several Midwest firms before joining the COLLECTORS' INFORMATION BUREAU in 1987. She currently resides in Grand Rapids, Michigan with her husband and two teenage children.

About the Writers

Susan K. Jones

Susan K. Jones has spent more than eighteen years in the limited edition collectibles field. She is the owner of Susan K. Jones and Associates, a consulting firm for direct marketers and limited edition marketers. She has been a Marketing Manager for The Hamilton Collection, and she worked with The Bradford Exchange in the mid-1970s.

Today Ms. Jones serves a number of collectibles clients and contributes to several collectibles publications. She authored *Creative Strategy in Direct Marketing* (NTC Business Books, 1991), and co-authored two business books published by Charles Scribner's Sons. Since 1990, Ms. Jones has served as an Associate Professor of Marketing at Ferris State University in Big Rapids, Michigan and has taught direct marketing at Northwestern University.

Ms. Jones was the first Executive Director of COLLECTORS' INFORMATION BUREAU and now serves as its Special Consultant. Ms. Jones' expertise in the collectibles field led her to write many of the company feature and background articles for this book.

Educated at Northwestern University, she holds a master's degree in advertising. She lives in East Grand Rapids, Michigan with her husband and two sons.

Catherine Bloom is a newspaper columnist and a writer for the COLLECTORS' INFORMATION BUREAU since 1983. She attended Loretto Heights College in Denver, Colorado and earned a bachelors degree from Creighton University in Omaha, Nebraska and her graduate studies were through The University of Michigan.

Ms. Bloom worked in the promotion departments of a number of radio and television stations in the Midwest. She currently lives in Grand Rapids, Michigan where her regular column "With Us Today" appears in the *Grand Rapids Press*.

In 1990, she did the text for *Capidomonte Collectibles*, published by Publications International, Inc. Since 1987, Ms. Bloom has also written the "C.I.B. Hotline" for *Collectors News*.

Ann Saigeon is a free-lance writer residing in Alto, Michigan. She was an adjunct professor of English at Calvin College in Grand Rapids, Michigan where she also has done research in publications for the art department. Ms. Saigeon's hobbies include gardening, travelling and Celtic studies.

A professional copy writer in the direct mail business for six years, Katherine Holden Trotti has also published magazine articles in such diverse publications as *New Woman, Collector Editions, Los Angeles Times Magazine* and *Palm Springs Life*. Her photographs have appeared in *Islands Magazine*. She lives in Santa Barbara, California.

Gail Cohen was introduced to the giftware/collectibles industry as trade show and sales and communications manager for The Bradford Exchange in 1980. In 1987, she became director of marketing for Roman, Inc., and in 1990 established The Gail Cohen Company, Inc., a full-service creative agency.

Ms. Cohen holds a masters degree in anthropology from the University of Georgia at Athens. Formerly a book reviewer for *The Library Journal*, her writings include articles for *Family Circle, Military Lifestyle, GSB, Northshore* (Chicago) and other magazines, as well as features in *The Chicago Tribune* and *The* (Chicagoland) *Daily Herald*.

Acknowledgments

The Collectors' Information Bureau would like to thank the following persons who have contributed to the creation of this book: Gail Cohen, Barbara Dike of Enesco Corporation, Ronald Frey of Interiors by Town & Country, Robert Groters of Klingman Furniture Company, Linda Joswick of Trade Typographers, Inc., Ray and Lorrie Kiefer of the National Association of Limited Edition Dealers, Todd Mellema of Philip B. Schaafsma Photography, Dan Nichols of Wm. C. Brown Publishers, Ann Saigeon, Philip Schaafsma of Philip B. Schaafsma Photography, Laurie Schaut and Carla Siegle of Trade Typographers, Inc., Pat Shaw of Enesco Corporation, John Spoelma of Klingman Furniture Company, Dave Stafford and Joy Versluys of Trade Typographers, Inc. and Katherine Holden Trotti.

In addition, the Collectors' Information Bureau would like to thank its panel of over one hundred limited edition dealers, whose dedication has helped make our ever-expanding 125 page-plus Price Index possible. We wish we could thank them by name, but they have agreed that to be singled out in this manner might hinder their continued ability to obtain an unbiased view of the marketplace.

The executive editor also wishes to express heartfelt appreciation to the following persons whose dedication, hard work and encouragement have made this book possible: Catherine P. Bloom, John Conley, Nancy Hart, Ron Jedlinski, Paul F. Jones, Susan K. Jones, Sue Knappen, Bruce Kollath, Heio W. Reich, Michelle Satterthwaite, James P. Smith, Jr., Carol Van Elderen and Cindy Zagumny.

By Heio W. Reich

President of COLLECTORS' INFORMATION BUREAU
and
President of RECO INTERNATIONAL CORP.

Foreword

Dear Collector:

It has been a decade since a group of dedicated collectibles marketers and producers met at the International Collectible Exposition in South Bend, Indiana. Their mission was to explore ideas for an important new means of communication with collectors. These visionary leaders foresaw an "information explosion" in the collectibles field. And they banded together to develop an organization that would be the "voice of the industry" serving collectors by sharing this growing body of information on limited editions.

That exploratory meeting led to more conferences, brainstorming and planning sessions. By November 1982—just four months after their initial meeting — the founders of COLLECTORS' INFORMATION BUREAU were ready to unveil their concept. Sponsored by a total of fourteen charter members, the COLLECTORS' INFORMATION BUREAU has now more than quadrupled its original membership with a Regular Members' roster that now includes 70 of the world's most honored marketers and manufacturers of fine art collectibles. Through the years, the BUREAU has expanded its services to collectors with the introduction of the "Collectibles Hotline" and the publishing of the "C.I.B. Report" Newsletter, the *Collectibles Price Guide* and its latest book, *Directory to Secondary Market Retailers*. This would not have been possible without the continued dedication and support of the CIB Board members, charter and regular member companies, secondary market retailers and countless others who have helped shape this dynamic organization. The CIB welcomes the numerous letters and phone calls it receives from enthusiastic collectors who enjoy their hobby, and thanks them for utilizing the CIB's resources.

The CIB was founded to be a direct link to collectors offering information on the most fascinating companies, artists, craftsmanship processes and product introductions in the world of limited editions. Even more important, the CIB pledged to create and publish an authoritative Price Index listing thousands of the most actively traded works of art in contemporary limited edition collecting. The initial medium for this information was to be a totally unique book: the first edition of what now is known as the COLLECTIBLES MARKET GUIDE & PRICE INDEX.

Our first GUIDE, published in 1984, contained 192 pages including a thirty-page Price Index. Today the COLLECTORS' INFORMATION BUREAU proudly presents the Tenth Edition of the COLLECTIBLES MARKET GUIDE & PRICE INDEX.

The GUIDE we introduce to you today comprises more than 575 pages, including an expanded 150-plus page Price Index that covers nearly 27,000 of today's most widely traded plates, figurines, bells, graphics, ornaments, dolls and steins.

Page through this comprehensive book and I feel sure you will agree it has become a "work of art" in and of itself. Our readers have praised the GUIDE as "The Collector's Bible" and "A Treasure Trove of Information." Novice collectors and seasoned veterans alike enjoy the GUIDE, which is based on recent developments, discoveries and events in the world of collectibles.

In these pages you will find historical perspectives on collecting plates, figurines, dolls and other limited edition categories…an up-to-date guide to the secondary market…ideas from a top interior designer on how to decorate your home with collectibles. You will also learn the best ways to protect your valuable holdings—both within your home and with insurance policies that guard against loss.

You will learn where to travel to see your favorite collectibles made, enjoy collectibles conventions and view noteworthy collections in museums and other exhibitions. And of course, there is the Price Index with its recent quote prices drawn from the combined experience of over 250 respected dealers all over North America.

So indulge yourself. Pour a cup of your favorite beverage and sit down prepared for a reading adventure! The members of COLLECTORS' INFORMATION BUREAU commend this volume to you as the latest edition of our authoritative book—devoted to enjoyment by you, the collector.

Cordially,

Heio W. Reich

Heio W. Reich
Port Washington, NY
November, 1992

Members

During its first year of existence, the CIB Membership Roster included fourteen member firms and six associate members. Today, the roster of member firms numbers seventy — an all-time record membership! Here is our current membership roster.

Kurt S. Adler, Inc./Santa's World
1107 Broadway
New York, NY 10010

Anheuser-Busch, Inc.
Retail Sales Department
2700 South Broadway
St. Louis, MO 63118

Annalee Mobilitee Dolls, Inc.
Box 708 Reservoir Road
Meredith, NH 03253

ANRI
c/o Goebel United States
Goebel Plaza
P.O. Box 10
Pennington, NJ 08534

Armani
c/o Miller Import
300 Mac Lane
Keasbey, Woodbridge
Township, NJ 08832

Artaffects, Ltd.
P.O. Box 98
Staten Island, NY 10307

The Ashton-Drake Galleries
9200 N. Maryland Avenue
Niles, IL 60648

The Bradford Exchange
9333 Milwaukee Avenue
Niles, IL 60648

Byers' Choice Ltd.
P.O. Box 158
Chalfont, PA 18914

The Cat's Meow
2163 Great Trails Drive
Wooster, OH 44691

**Classic Carolina Collections/
C.U.I., Inc./DRAM TREE**
1502 North 23rd Street
Wilmington, NC 28405

The Collectables
Rt. 4, Box 503
Rolla, MO 65401

The Constance Collection
Rte 1, Box 538
Midland, VA 22728

M. Cornell Importers, Inc.
1462- 18th Street N.W.
St. Paul, MN 55112

Corolle/Timeless Creations
333 Continental Blvd.
El Segundo, CA 90245-5012

Creart
4517 Manzanillo Drive
Austin, TX 78749

Cross Gallery
P.O. Box 4181
Jackson Hole, WY 83001

Department 56, Inc.
PO Box 44456
Eden Prairie, MN 55344-1456

The Walt Disney Company
500 South Buena Vista Street
Burbank, CA 91521

Duncan Royale
1141 So. Acacia Avenue
Fullerton, CA 92631

Dynasty Doll
P.O. Box 99
400 Markley Street
Port Reading, NJ 07064

Enesco Corporation
1 Enesco Plaza
Elk Grove Village, IL 60007

Flambro Imports
1260 Collier Road N.W.
Atlanta, GA 30318

The Franklin Mint
U.S. Route One
Franklin Center, PA 19091

Gartlan USA, Inc.
15502 Graham Street
Huntington Beach, CA 92649

Georgetown Collection
One Foden Rd.
Portland, ME 04104-5030

Goebel United States
Goebel Plaza
P.O. Box 10
Pennington, NJ 08534-0010

Goebel Miniatures
c/o Goebel United States
P.O. Box 10, Rt. 31
Pennington, NJ 08534

Gorham Inc.*
P.O. Box 2011
Penndel, PA 19047

The Hamilton Collection*
4810 Executive Park Court
Jacksonville, FL 32216-6069

Hand & Hammer Silversmiths
Hand & Hammer Collectors' Club
2610 Morse Lane
Woodbridge, VA 22192

John Hine Studios, Inc.
4456 Campbell Road
P.O. Box 800667
Houston, TX 77280-0667

M.I. Hummel Club*
Division of Goebel Art GmbH
Goebel Plaza
P.O. Box 11
Pennington, NJ 08534-0011

Kaiser Porcelain USA Inc.
2045 Niagara Falls Blvd.
Niagara Falls, NY 14304

Ladie & Friends, Inc.
220 North Main Street
Sellersville, PA 18960

Lance Corporation
321 Central Street
Hudson, MA 01749

Lawtons
548 North First
Turlock, CA 95380

Ron Lee's World of Clowns
2180 Agate Court
Simi Valley, CA 93065

LEGENDS
2665D Park Center Drive
Simi Valley, CA 93065

Lenox Collections
1170 Wheeler Way
Langhorne, PA 19047

Lightpost Publishing
Ten Almaden Blvd. 9th Floor
San Jose, CA 95113

Lilliput Lane Limited
c/o Gift Link, Inc.
9052 Old Annapolis Road
Columbia, MD 21045

Lladro Collectors Society
43 W. 57th Street
New York, NY 10019

Seymour Mann, Inc.
225 Fifth Avenue,
Showroom #102
New York, NY 10010

Maruri U.S.A.
7541 Woodman Place
Van Nuys, CA 91405

June McKenna Collectibles Inc.
P.O. Box 846
Ashland, VA 23005

**Midwest Importers of
Cannon Falls, Inc.**
P.O. Box 20, Consumer Inquiries
Cannon Falls, MN 55009-0020

Nahrgang Collection
1005 First Avenue
Silvis, IL 61282

Novelino, Inc.
12-A Mason
Irvine, CA 92718

PenDelfin Sales Inc.
750 Ensminger Road,
Suite 108
Tonawanda, NY 14150

Polland Studios
P.O. Box 1146
Prescott, AZ 86302

Possible Dreams
6 Perry Dr.
Foxboro, MA 02035

Precious Art/Panton
110 E. Ellsworth Road
Ann Arbor, MI 48108

Reco International Corp.*
150 Haven Avenue
Port Washington, NY 11050

The Norman Rockwell Gallery
9200 Center for the Arts
Niles, IL 60648

Roman, Inc.*
555 Lawrence Avenue
Roselle, IL 60172-1599

**Royal Copenhagen/Bing &
Grondahl**
27 Holland Ave.
White Plains, NY 10603

Royal Doulton
700 Cottontail Lane
Somerset, NJ 08873

Sarah's Attic
126-1/2 West Broad
Chesaning, MI 48616

Schmid
55 Pacella Park Drive
Randolph, MA 02368

Silver Deer, Ltd.
4824 Sterling Drive
Boulder, CO 80301

Summerhill Crystal & Glass
P.O. Box 1479
Fairfield, IA 52556

Swarovski America Ltd.
2 Slater Road
Cranston, RI 02920

Takara
230 Fifth Avenue,
New York, NY 10001

Timeless Creations
333 Continental Blvd.
El Segundo, CA 90245-5012

Turner Dolls Inc.
P.O. Box 36
Heltonville, IN 47436

United Design
P.O. Box 1200
Noble, OK 73068

VickiLane, Inc.
515 Colonial Dr.
Springfield, OR 97477

WACO Products Corporation
One North Corporate Drive
Riverdale, NJ 07457

Charter Member

———— Associate Members ————

Custom China Creations
13726 Seminole Drive
Chino, CA 91710

Mattheyprint Corporation
1397 King Road
West Chester, PA 16105

The Joy of Collecting
American Collectors Share Their Enthusiasm for Limited Edition Plates, Figurines, Bells, Graphics, Ornaments and Dolls

Unique home decor...the lure of the chase...a retirement pastime...an investment for the future. These are but a few of the reasons why today's collectors enjoy their beautiful limited editions. Their motives are as varied as their collections, but these enthusiasts have at least one thing in common: they love their beautiful works of art.

To gain insight into the strong and steady growth of the limited edition field, Collectors' Information Bureau interviewed male and female collectors from every U.S. region, age group and walk of life. Here we share the highlights of this fascinating survey.

It wouldn't be Christmas without Sandi Hight's doll collection, which is attractively displayed throughout the Hight home during the holidays. A large Annalee Mobilitee Santa makes himself comfortable on the family piano bench, while other Annalee dolls sing holiday favorites.

The Inspiration to Collect

Some collectors insist that the hobby is "in their blood" — a passion that was passed down to them by parents or grandparents who filled their childhood homes with cherished objects. Others knew nothing of collecting until a special friend or relative gave them a gift: a plate, bell or figurine that turned out to be a limited edition.

Michael G. Brennan of Cherry Hill, New Jersey claims he "married into a family of collectors." While visiting shops that sold the Bing and Grondahl and Royal Copenhagen plates enjoyed by his wife and mother-in-law, David Winter's charming cottages caught Brennan's eye. Now he says of the David Winter line, "They have become a passion with me. I greatly admire the uniqueness and artistry that goes into each and every cottage."

Dara Bise of Crossville, Tennessee received a Precious Moments "Time Heals" figurine instead of flowers after major surgery, from a sister-in-law who loves Sam Butcher's heartwarming designs. Karin Warner of Christianburg, Virginia, was already a raccoon collector when her mother purchased several collectible raccoons for her as gifts. Now Ms. Warner collects every raccoon she can find in the form of plates, figurines, graphics, and even ornaments.

Like Ms. Warner, many collectors become intrigued when they discover a collector's item that ties in with a favorite subject. As a Shrine clown, Frank Yetner of Warwick, Rhode Island became an admirer and collector of Duncan Royale figurines and other clown-subject works.

A love of "The Nutcracker" ballet spurred Donna Arthur's collecting hobby in Rowland Heights, California, while Diane K. McCarrick first discovered plate collecting when she learned her favorite comedian, Red Skelton, would attend the International Plate and Collectible Exposition in South Bend, Indiana. Ms. McCarrick traveled to the South Bend show from her home in Lansing, Michigan in 1977, and has attended each annual convention since. "We went to see Red Skelton, but once I stepped on that floor, I was hooked," she explains. Now Ms. McCarrick owns works by Lowell Davis, Swarovski, Lladro, and many other collectibles firms.

Fran Oldrigde uses two stunning Lalique crystal cats to accessorize her end table.

This is just a small sampling of Karin Warner's ever-growing raccoon collection! Attractively displayed are Roger Brown's "Reggie," Maruri USA raccoon, Schmid's "Coon Capers Moonraiders" by Lowell Davis, "Bobby Coon" by Goebel, Schmid's "Anybody's Home," by Lowell Davis, "Ruffles" by Cybis, Boehm Studios' raccoon and Lowell Davis' "Creek Bank Bandit."

Joyce Lambert displays her cottages in aquariums. "My cottages are dust-free and away from children's little hands as long as they are in the aquarium." There is a David Winter emblem at the top of the aquarium, etched by Joyce's son.

The Fun of Sharing a Collection

The collectors we surveyed agreed that home display is one of the most rewarding aspects of their pastime. Their decor ideas abound all year long, but their Christmas displays are especially elaborate. Beverly A. Thyssen of Little Chute, Wisconsin uses her dolls and teddy bears for a Christmas display in her front bay window. She combines "Mr. and Mrs. Claus, elves, dolls and bears. Cars actually stop to look," she reports proudly.

Even her normally skeptical sons insist that Sandi Hight decorate their Skowhegan, Maine home with all the holiday collectibles she has gathered. "My two boys are always having a fit about dolls being all over the house," she smiles. "So one year I decided not to decorate so extensively. About the second week into December my boys said, 'Aren't we having Christmas?'" It goes without saying that Ms. Hight then "decked the halls" with all her seasonal Annalee Dolls and Hallmark Merry Miniatures.

Although Billie Lou Frandsen of Rock Springs, Wyoming started out wanting only a simple village scene to place under her Christmas tree, she and her whole family have become Department 56 enthusiasts. "I enjoy putting a large village scene on the entertainment center," she says. "We have two cobblestone 'roads' with street lights and our favorite pieces, lots of snow and people. Trees and coaches also decorate the scene." As of this writing, Ms. Frandsen owned 56 buildings, seven coaches and sleighs, and scores of people, trees, animals and street lights for her grand holiday display.

Christmas isn't the only time for decoration, however, and Joyce Lambert of Coal Grove, Ohio has devised a clever way to show off her cottage collection all year long. "I have three 20-gallon aquariums that I display my cottages in," she explains. "The aquariums are stacked and have a light on top to shine down through the tanks." A unique display indeed!

Fran Oldridge of Anaheim Hills, California treasures her two Lalique crystal cat sculptures above all other possessions. "My Lalique cats are on a lamp table between my sofa and loveseat," she says. "People — myself included — who sit on the end of the sofa or loveseat usually end up stroking or 'petting' the cats as they talk, unaware of what they are doing!"

People with extensive collections often plan their furniture arrangements with display in mind. The owner of 250 collector plates, Inez B. Tillison of Atlanta, Georgia has a twelve-foot-long shelf in her living room especially for her Bjorn Wiinblad plates. "We also have a china cabinet full," she adds.

Georgiana Bodemer of Green Brook, New Jersey houses her collectibles on shelves and glassed-in cabinets. "It keeps them so clean and new looking," she exclaims. Ms. Bodemer has two large collector's cabinets and one attorney's book case in which to store her favorite works of art. And a roll-top desk plays host to Quinn Dahlstrom's Krystonia dragons and English miniature cottages in Bonney Lake, Washington.

A Never-Ending Passion for Collecting

Our collector "panel" tells us that their enjoyment of limited editions has no bounds. Some people who collect the works of a certain artist or firm are spurred on to acquire the newest items in that line. Others enjoy seeking out back issues or rare pieces — some even call or travel all over the country looking for special treasures.

Still others find collecting is a wonderful way to fill spare hours — either during their retirement years or as a happy diversion from the world of work. Florence Zulick of Hazel Park, Michigan goes so far as to call her collecting hobby "great therapy in times when life held many disappointments."

The comments and encouragement of friends and relatives spur on some collectors, as Rose Patterson knows. Ms. Patterson, of San Pedro, California, says that "When family and friends come to my home, the first thing they say is how warm and cozy it feels to be there. I know that a lot of that has to do with my different collections."

Barbara Ann Hart, a doll collector in La Porte, Texas, says that friends "tease me about my 'babies,' but they always ask about what I'm watching for (to acquire) and have surprised me many times with new additions."

The Importance of a Good Dealer

Many collectors prefer selecting a special dealer whose shop they can visit, and who alerts them

Georgiana Bodemer's collectibles are stored safely in glassed-in cabinets. She uses the back wall in the case to hang some of her pieces, as well as the ornaments that hang from the shelves themselves. This technique adds interest to her arrangement and gives Georgiana more space to work with.

Quinn Bahlstrom arranges his fantasy figurines and cottages in a cozy setting. From left to right are "Owhey" from Precious Art/Panton, "Secret Garden" from Lilliput Lane, "Stoope" from Precious Art/Panton and "Hometown Depot" from Lilliput Lane.

Two husband and wife teams take great joy at arranging their Department 56 villages for the holidays. Above, Billie Lou Frandsen and her husband put their favorite and/or newest pieces in front to construct a main road and continue creating the village from there. Shown left, is just a partial collection of a Department 56 village as displayed by Florence Zulick and her husband, whose entire collection spans three walls. The village is displayed from late October until February.

Edith Smith poses with a few of her David Winter cottages. She enjoys looking for retired pieces and plans to continue collecting them until she runs out of space to show them!

when new collectibles come on the market. Dealers who feature favorite artists at get-togethers and signing parties win high marks from their customers, as do firms that buy and sell on the secondary market. Indeed, while few of our survey respondents buy mainly for investment purposes, they do like to know that there is an outlet available if they ever should wish to participate in secondary market trading.

Other collectors enjoy purchasing collectibles by mail for a number of reasons: selection, convenience, and payment terms, to name a few.

Toni Meyer of Wausau, Wisconsin says she buys "a lot of collectibles by mail, because I cannot always find what I'm looking for in town. I buy from advertisements, and I get retired pieces from collectible exchanges."

As a senior citizen, Doris M. Foster of Telford, Pennsylvania likes the convenience of buying from home. And Judy Anderson of Mukwonago, Wisconsin appreciates the mail-order policy of installment buying, which allows her to spread her payments.

Collectors Share Their Joy of Collecting

When asked what special comments they would like to share with fellow collectors, our respon-dents were most eloquent. Philip L. Field of Norwalk, Connecticut finds collecting to be "educational, profitable, and a wonderful pastime for rainy or winter days."

Edith Smith of Richmond, Virginia compares collecting to an addiction or habit — "except it is a wonderful one that can be enjoyed for years to come. It is one of the great joys of my life."

Rita K. Clark of Salinas, California appreciates the monetary value of her favorite pieces as well as their appeal. "Through collecting things I love for their beauty and artistry, I always have my money's worth. But knowing their values — some of which are growing — gives me a wonderful sense of security."

Collectibles and Your Home Design
A Top Interior Designer's Advice Sparks New Ideas for Showing Off Your Favorite Works of Limited Edition Art

Imagine a living room furnished in neutral tones with wall-to-wall carpet, white painted walls, a sofa, two pull-up chairs, coffee table and floor lamps. Sounds functional...even comfortable. But charming? Inviting? Not really. A room may be fitted with all the basics of seating and lighting, but without accessories and a few special touches of personality and style, it remains as cold and impersonal as a public waiting area!

We all sense the difference between a "ho-hum room" and one that sings with joy and warmth. But few of us possess a natural flair for home design: we need the advice of an expert to turn our favorite rooms into cozy retreats that are sought out happily by family and friends. Nothing adds personal style to a room more effectively that one's carefully chosen plates, bells, figurines, graphics, ornaments and dolls. But some collectors are unsure as to how to display their treasures for maximum enjoyment and beauty. That's why Collectors' Information Bureau has enlisted the guidance of Interior Designer Ronald Frey.

Ronald Frey

A member of the American Society of Interior Designers (A.S.I.D.), Frey is certified by the National Council for Interior Design Qualification (NCIDQ) — and he is listed in the current International Edition of Barons *Who's Who In Interior Design*. Based in Allendale, Michigan at Interiors by Town & Country, Frey holds a B.F.A. in Interior Design from the renowned Kendall College of Art and Design in Grand Rapids, Michigan, and is a member of Kendall's adjunct faculty. In an exclusive interview with C.I.B. Special Consultant Susan K. Jones, Frey shared his authoritative tips on adorning the home with collectibles.

Even Novices Can Design With Style

At one time home design was constrained by certain musts, but according to Ronald Frey, "There are no longer any rules for displaying objets d'art — only that the display be executed with taste."

Frey cautions, however, that working without rules does not mean that "anything goes."

"The trained eye will be able to discern problem areas immediately. But for the person with little or no training in design, a few suggestions on displaying collectibles may be of help."

This oriental plate rail from Van Hygan & Smythe demonstrates an excellent way to attractively display many plates in a limited space.

Be Aware of Scale. "Relating the size of an object to the space around it is very important," Frey cautions. "The obvious mistake to avoid here is displaying too small an item in too large a space, or vice-versa. Think of proportion: relating one part to another, each part to the whole, and each object to the other objects."

Frey says that some especially interesting, unique and imposing items may be strong enough

Swarovski crystal ornaments and train create an elegance at Chrismas time, that collectors will certainly admire. The ornaments hang attractively on a tree trimmed with bows, while a Swarovski train sits on a track that encircles the tree.

to stand alone and become focal elements in the room. A large sculpture of a bird or animal, for instance, might command its surrounding space while a smaller wildlife sculpture would need to be grouped with other items.

How To Unify Collectibles in Groups. When grouping items together, Frey suggests that you find some way to relate each piece to the overall display. "For example, one approach I take is to place different objects with similar colors together for harmony. Or, I may place objects of varying heights side by side for contrast and variation."

Frey suggests that when showing a group of objects that differ in size, an asymmetrical composition is best. On the other hand, pieces of the same size look well when combined in a straight row, or stacked above and below each other.

Using the Design Principle of Rhythm. According to Frey, "When you repeat elements either by size, texture or color to form a regular pattern, you employ the concept of rhythm. A properly composed and balanced display, whether symmetrical or asymmetrical, will naturally seem correct because the objects will achieve a 'state of being' in which they equal each other."

The key is to avoid haphazard placement of objects, yet take a risk from time to time. "Crystal objects can take on a very avant garde look when displayed in a straight line at a further than normal distance from each other," Frey suggests. Of course, some collectors may still prefer to show off their crystal pieces in a more traditional cluster on a tabletop or curio cabinet shelf.

Experiment With Eclectic Displays. Ronald Frey encourages collectors to mix and match items whose periods and "statements" are totally unrelated — antique pieces with contemporary works of art, for example, or child-subject works mixed with wildlife pieces. "This is one of my most fun and favorite things to do," Frey explains.

"On a tabletop, for instance, mix and layer items of different heights from back to front. Remember to unify all the items in some way — perhaps harmonizing colors. Though this is challenging, when it's executed correctly, this type of mix can lead to a visually surprising room that awakens every one of the human senses."

A Wide Range of Areas for Display. "There are many different places to display collections," according to Ronald Frey. "Two or three pieces combined with a few art books, some magazines and a plant or cut flowers in a vase make for a stunning cocktail table," he believes. "Other tables and

Doll artist Phyllis Parkins decorates her home, using many of her own lovely dolls as accents. Pictured is "Kallie," the second collector club exclusive from Phyllis' Collectors Club. The wall grouping of three child-subject graphics adds to this lovely setting.

desktops can combine photos, pottery, ornaments, plates, paintings and candlesticks — all of which do *not* have to match.

"Bookshelves are excellent pedestals for smaller objects and look very charming when their contents are mixtures of books, periodicals and items of display. And try this: by painting the back of the bookcase black or another dark color, the elements on display seem to pop out at you for notice."

Try displaying the same artist's works, but in different forms, as shown here. Sandra Kuck's artwork is attractively displayed, with "Afternoon Recital" appropriately set upon this collector's piano, while Ms. Kuck's "The Reading Lesson" graphic by V.F. Fine Arts completes this charming scene.

More "Homes" for Collectibles. "Armoires with glass doors and shelves, lit from above, become dramatic settings for collections of all kinds," Ronald Frey suggests. "Use the tops of armoires and bookcases for additional display for special objects. Use walls for mounting photos, graphics and other artworks. These are particularly interesting when placed in a low position to create a more intimate feeling. Deep window sills and even the floor are other perfect areas to stack and prop things."

The Importance of Lighting. Frey emphasizes good lighting above all else in creating a handsome home. "I could utilize everything mentioned above, yet without the proper lighting, displays die quickly," he cautions. "There are a hundred different solutions to lighting, all correct, yet the one I come back to again and again for collections is the

Many collectors display their favorite holiday ornaments all year long. Above: Hallmark wooden ornament trees house miniature ornaments. Below: This angel collection is shown on a folding white metal display rack, with ribbon woven throughout to soften the setting.

Several M.I. Hummel figurines were used to create this lovely vignette.

pinspot or narrow spot. Used in a recessed incandescent fixture or with a small, unobtrusive track fixture, these low-voltage, tungsten-halogen lamps will thrust narrow beams of light with great precision. The result is an exciting and dramatic look, with dark shadows surrounding the objects that are highlighted."

Frey borrowed this lighting concept from his retail designs, where he focuses intense beams of light on featured objects. "It works in residential design as well, and why shouldn't we have as much fun in our homes as when we go shopping?" Another tip from Frey: use reostats to vary the intensity of light depending on the time of day and the effect you seek.

Have Fun and Be Daring. Ronald Frey's final word of advice concerns "taking the plunge" with your home display and showing off those offbeat objects that say "you." "Many times the items I select as accessories for my clients are objects they currently own and just never considered. I find them stored away somewhere because they were thought of as 'old' or 'inappropriate.' The main thing to remember is to have fun, be daring, and take the risk to display some objects you like in a creative way. When you do this, you can only enhance the collectibles you are displaying!"

Here are some specific ideas for each of the collectible categories featured in this book:

Plates

* Try hanging four or more plates of the same size in a straight vertical line — one on top of the other.
* Mix plates on a theme with other objects that amplify that theme: Victorian lace, a children's tea cup and saucer and a fairy tale book with a nostalgic, child-subject plate for example.
* Show off your plates in every room of the home: including the bathroom and kitchen. Porcelain is the ideal art medium for these rooms because it is durable and easy to clean.
* Today's plate frames add elegance and style to porcelain art. Try rustic oak frames for plates in the family room...polished dark wood frames for the living room.

Figurines and Bells

* Add interest to a display by placing some pieces on pedestals to vary their heights.
* Keep your finest and most delicate figurines and bells safe and clean by investing in a lighted glass cabinet or shelving unit.
* Christmas pieces may be displayed all year: don't limit your enjoyment to just a few weeks annually.
* Add a favorite piece or two to your bedroom, or rotate figurines and bells from your living room to your private quarters: you'll enjoy waking up to beauty each day!

Dolls

* There's nothing more charming than a child-size chair or rocker adorned by one or more pretty dolls
* Let your porcelain "babies" slumber in a real baby's cradle or wicker basket
* If you own a number of elegant lady dolls, set up a child-size table, chairs and tea set for a tea party vignette
* A standing doll shows off her costume to best advantage: many contemporary dolls come with their own unobtrusive stands at no additional charge

Graphics

* White walls serve as a complementary backdrop for a large collection of graphics in different sizes and varied frames
* Group graphics and collector plates for an eclectic look; unify them by theme or style
* If you enjoy traditional decor, try hanging your graphics Victorian style with ribbons, or with wires suspended from the crown molding
* Consider frames as carefully as you do the graphics you choose: a handsome frame can double the impact of a work of art

Ornaments

* Don't be afraid to decorate more than one Christmas tree: many ornament collectors now boast a tree for every room of the home at holiday time!
* Show off some of your favorite ornaments all year 'round: suspend them from hooks and hangers to brighten rooms no matter what the season
* When you "deck the halls" with pine boughs, add some of your favorite ornaments to the display
* Carefully chosen ornaments make a pretty centerpiece when piled in a crystal bowl

The Secondary Market
Leading Dealers Share Their Hard-Won Knowledge About Buying and Selling Collectibles on the Secondary Market

I recently overheard a well-known collectibles producer bemoaning the fact that one of his loveliest plates would never see significant secondary market action. "We introduced it in a limited edition of just 1,000," the gentleman explained, "and so few people have ever heard of it or seen it that it has never penetrated the market"!

Imagine that: a limited-edition collectible whose edition is *too small* to ensure its opportunity for secondary market price rises! Novices in the field would be sure to surmise just the opposite: aren't we all taught from childhood that the rarer an item is, the more likely it is to appreciate in value?

The fact is that in today's international collectibles market, with millions of enthusiastic art lovers vying to own the most popular works, a piece with a relatively large edition may well "outperform" an extremely limited plate, figurine or other collectible. Why? Because the key to the market is supply and demand.

If available supply is less than pent-up demand for a given work of art, that piece's price most often will begin to climb on the auction market. Demand cannot be stimulated without collectors' knowledge of the item's existence. And those items which are seen throughout the marketplace are most likely to attract and sustain the interest of a broad range of collectors.

This short "object lesson" is meant to illustrate a point. Today's market for limited edition collectibles is complex, exciting and fast-paced. And its patterns of success do not necessarily "square" with a collector's experience in financial markets or other aspects of life.

There is a great deal to learn and understand in order to make the best buying and selling decisions. And to gather this valuable knowledge for our readers, Collectors' Information Bureau has interviewed more than 20 top limited edition dealers who are actively involved in today's secondary market for plates, figurines, bells, graphics, ornaments and dolls.

What Is the Secondary Market?

To begin, let us establish the step-by-step process by which a limited edition collectible enters the secondary market.

1. A collectible is introduced to the market and made available to collectors. Collectors may purchase the item through a dealer (in person or by mail or phone), or direct from the manufacturer/marketer (usually by mail or phone only). Items are sold at "original issue price," which is their retail price level. This method of selling is known as the "primary market."

2. After a period which may vary from days to years, the collectible becomes "sold out." This means that neither the dealers nor the manufacturer/marketers have any additional pieces to sell to collectors on the primary market.

3. When a collector wishes to buy a piece which is "sold out," he or she must enter the "secondary market" to purchase it. Because the piece is no longer available at retail, the new buyer must locate someone who already owns it and pay whatever price the market will bear. Most buyers enlist the help of a dealer, exchange, or matching service to help them in this process, while some place want ads in collectibles publications, or "network" with fellow collectors.

4. If new buyers continue to seek to acquire the piece long after its edition is sold out, the secondary market for that item may become stronger

Going Once, Going Twice — This doll auction in Plymouth, Michigan, conducted by International Doll Exhibitions and Auctions Ltd. and sponsored by Georgia's Gift Gallery, was part of an all-day event attended by over 2,500 doll enthusiasts.

and stronger and the price it can command may multiply over and over. Such market action is reported in the Collectors' Information Bureau Price Index at the back of this book.

Of course, some collectibles never sell out completely, while others sell out but never attract sufficient demand to command a higher price than the issue-price level. Some collectibles peak soon after their editions close, while others remain dormant for years and then begin rising in value because of changing market dynamics.

Manufacturers, dealers, and collectibles experts alike caution all collectors to *buy items that they like and want to display*, without regard for possible price rises. No one knows for certain whether a given item will end up rising in value on the secondary market.

How Collectible Editions are Limited

The term "limited edition" is one that many collectors find confusing, since studios limit production of their collectibles in many different ways. Here is an explanation of the most common methods of edition limitation.

Limited by Number: The producer sets a worldwide edition limit which may be a round number, or a number with special significance. Gartlan U.S.A., for example, often limits its sports collectibles to numbers that have importance in the careers of the sports celebrities they depict. Such items may carry their own sequential numbers within the edition.

Limited by Time: The producer pledges to craft an item only during a specific time period: the year 1992, for instance. A Christmas plate might close its edition on Christmas Eve of the year of issue, as another example. Or a commemorative figurine might be offered for the two years prior to a historic event, then close its edition on the date of the event. Such items may carry their own sequential numbers within the edition.

Limited by Firing Period: This designation has to do with the number of items that can be kiln-fired by a marketer or producer in a given number of days. It is stated in terms such as "limited to a total of 14 firing days." Items limited by firing period most often are sequentially numbered on the backstamp or bottomstamp.

Limited to Members: In recent years, many collectibles clubs have offered "members-only" items that are available only during a set time period, and only to individuals who have joined the club. A secondary market for these items develop when individuals join the club in later years and wish to acquire earlier editions of "members-only" collecti-

bles that are no longer available at retail.

Open Editions that are Closed or Retired: While open editions are not strictly considered limited editions, they may stimulate secondary market action when they are closed or retired, and are no longer available at original-issue price.

Advice to Collectors Entering the Secondary Market

Deciding how to go about buying and selling on the secondary market, and what "philosophy of collecting" to adopt can be challenging to collectors. Here, some words of wisdom from experienced dealers provide guidelines to new and seasoned collectors.

When considering the sale of an item, the first step is to "determine the present secondary market value of the collectible," according to Lynda Blankenship of Dickens' Exchange in Metairie, Louisiana. Ms. Blankenship advises collectors to check this book or monthly update reports in collectibles magazines for prices. "Or contact a secondary broker for an opinion," she suggests.

Being realistic in setting a price is important, says Bob Phillips of The Wishing Well in Solvang, California. "Don't think that your piece is worth more than the other person's or you'll be hanging onto it longer than you want," Phillips cautions. Sandie Ellis of Ellis in Wonderland, Sacramento, California, echoes his advice and adds a comment of her own. "If you are looking for a quick sale, set the price below market; otherwise be prepared to wait," she says.

Sometimes a buyer is waiting in the wings in your own "back yard," according to Reda Walsh of The Kent Collection in Englewood, Colorado. That's why Ms. Walsh advises collectors to "check with your local retail dealer first to see if they are looking" for the item or items you have to sell. Another possibility, according to Marge Rosenberg of Carol's Gift Shop, Artesia, California, is selling through a local collectors club. "Most of them have Swap and Sell events at their meetings," she explains.

In setting prices, collectors should understand that the amount they clear from the sale of an item will depend upon how they arrange to sell it. The prices quoted in most price guides — including the one at the back of this book — are retail prices. Any brokerage fees, commissions, consignment fees or cost of ads will be deducted from this price. What's more, price quotes represent averages: an item may command more at certain times and in certain areas of the country and less in others depending upon supply and demand.

In addition, price quotes assume that the item is perfect — in mint condition. Chips, repairs, discolorations, production flaws, damage, or other imperfections will negatively impact the selling price in most cases. As the seller, you should be straightforward about your collectible's condition, says Patricia M. Cantrell of Village Realty Miniature Properties, Fort Worth, Texas. "If any problems are found, they should be noted and the prospective buyer made aware of them," she cautions.

Sandy Forgach of Collectibles etc., Inc. Match Service and Gift Shop says that cleaning one's collectibles before selling them will help maximize the price they can command. "People often make no effort to clean them," Ms. Forgach says, but a dusty and dingy piece is much less likely to bring a top price than one which is mint-condition clean.

Making Smooth Buying Transactions on the Secondary Market

In addition to the often-heard advice to "buy only what you like," experienced dealers have much to share in the way of guidelines for secondary market buyers. Their most frequent comment is to be sure that you know whom you are dealing with: the choice of a broker, buy-sell service or other "go-between" is often even more important for the buyer than it is for the seller.

Sandy Forgach suggests paying with a charge card when you buy from an ad. This offers you protection in case the item is not in mint condition or does not arrive as promised. "When you pay by check, you assume all the risks," she explains.

Connie Eckman of Collectible Exchange Inc. in New Middletown, Ohio, advises collectors to buy only the items they need to fill in collections they're working on. She has found that people who purchase an item only in the hopes that it will rise in value — so they can sell at a profit — are often disappointed. "Speculating at secondary prices rarely pays off," she says.

"Don't just shop in your own back yard," says Linda Blankenship. Take advantage of possible regional differences in price by checking around. "If a piece is constantly available at the same price, it is obviously not a fabulous deal," Ms. Blankenship continues. Education, patience and staying abreast of the market will yield the best possible bargain, she believes.

Those who plan on buying via the secondary market should "go on mailing lists of as many reputable secondary market dealers as possible," says Becky Flynn of Dollsville Dolls and Bearsville Bears in Palm Springs, California. This will enable the collector to research items just by reading over the mail they receive.

While there is some controversy over the necessity of obtaining boxes, certificates and other materials that originally accompanied the collectible, it is in the buyer's best interest to receive this material if at all possible. In this case, an experienced and reputable dealer or broker can be of help in determining what came with the collectible upon its arrival from the producer. "Be certain all necessary papers, Certificates of Authenticity, etc. are available at the time of purchase," says Karen Wilson of Callahan's of Calabash Nautical Gifts, Calabash, North Carolina.

Finally, a collector should rationally assess what a piece is worth to him or her, and make buying decisions accordingly. In the heat of an auction situation, collectors may bid a piece up to 20 or 30 times its original price, and still be happy to get it. Other collectors are more conservative, perhaps to their later regret. As Renee Tyler of Collector's Marketplace in Montrose, Pennsylvania says, "I've seen people miss a great chance to get something special because of a $25.00 difference in price."

The C.I.B. Price Index Offers a Starting Point for Secondary Prices

As our experts have said, one good first step to take before buying or selling a collectible is to

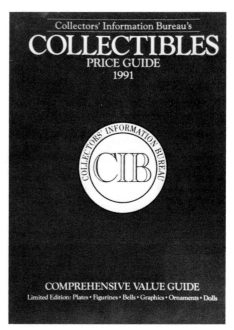

The first step before buying or selling a collectible is to check its recent price quote from a reliable source such as the Collectors' Information Bureau's Collectibles Price Guide.

check on its recent quote price from one or more reliable sources. To get started, check the Collectors' Information Bureau Price Index in the back of this book. It's the most comprehensive Price Index for limited edition plates, figurines, bells, graphics, ornaments and dolls available in the marketplace today!

As with any Price Index, a collector must look upon secondary information as a guide and not the value of an item right down to the penny. Some collectibles retain the same value for years, while others rise or fall faster than the information is printed.

The Collectors' Information Bureau Price Index is prepared very carefully. Manufacturers supply all pertinent product information to the C.I.B. This data is then entered into a computer. Copies of the Price Index are then mailed to our panel of dealers located all across the country. These knowledgeable store owners report actual selling prices back to the C.I.B. headquarters.

As mentioned above, collectibles may sell for different prices throughout the country. Therefore, a price or a price range is determined for each entry based upon careful analysis of the dealer reports. The Price Index is printed for this book and also updated one more time during the year.

Should collectors ever question a secondary market quote, they are advised to seek a second source or to write to the Collectors' Information Bureau for an updated value.

Collectors can place buy and sell orders for limited edition plates by calling The Bradford Exchange's Trading Floor.

Specific Ways to Buy and Sell Collectibles

Experts recommend several avenues for the collector who wishes to buy or sell a collectible once it is sold out at the retail level. Here are details on each procedure.

Contact the Manufacturer. While most manufacturers consider it unethical to directly determine their products' secondary market values, they may offer services to interested collectors who would otherwise find it difficult to purchase or sell a collectible on the secondary market.

Such services may include listings or ads in a company or club newsletter or publication, a matching service which helps prospective buyers and sellers make contact, or referrals to dealers who are actively involved in trading the firm's collectibles. In addition, some manufacturers help arrange for auctions at which collectors or club members may offer their pieces for sale to the highest bidder. Results of these auctions then may be reported in company or club newsletters.

Place a Classified Ad. Collectors may elect to place a classified ad in a collector publication to avoid paying a commission to a third party. The cost of the ad will be deducted from the profit, but if a collector sells directly to another collector, the seller can normally expect to receive a value closer to an item's secondary market quote price. Refer to the listing of "Magazines and Newsletters" elsewhere in this book for publications to contact.

According to Cherie Henn of *Collectors News*, the more details that appear in the ad, the more likely it is that a transaction will result. She suggests including a specific price you are willing to pay or to accept, along with a phone number instead of or in addition to an address. If you are responding to an ad, promptness is essential, as both buyers and sellers are anxious to proceed once the ad is in print.

The Bradford Exchange. Bradford is a long-established exchange for buyers and sellers of limited edition plates only. The Exchange acts as an agent for its clients, and guarantees that the trader-seller will be paid. Bradford also guarantees that the buyer will receive a plate in mint condition with proper certification. The Exchange acts as a broker to ensure trustworthy and fair transactions.

There is no fee for listing a plate on the Exchange, but a thirty percent fee will be subtracted from the sale price when a plate is sold. These sales are recorded and maintained on a computer to provide information about secondary market sales. Collectors can place buy and sell orders simply by calling the Exchange's toll-free number for the Trading Floor at 1-800-323-8078.

Retail Dealers. There are many dealers and store owners across the country who will work with collectors interested in selling their collectibles. Some dealers will work with regular customers to make trades if the dealer needs what the collector has, permitting them to trade up to a more valuable or newer item. Others may offer to take items on consignment. Since each dealer operates differently, collectors should expect policies to vary.

Another avenue for buying or selling collectibles is through retail dealers who specialize in the secondary market.

Our survey of dealers revealed that they charge commissions and brokerage fees ranging from 5% to 35%. While in most cases the seller absorbs this cost, it is sometimes split between the buyer and the seller. Shipping and insurance costs are another matter: they may be paid by the seller, split by buyer and seller, or in rare cases, absorbed by the dealer out of his/her commission. Sometimes the dealer takes the item into possession and displays it in the shop until it is sold. In other cases, the seller retains the item until a bargain is made.

Some dealers prefer to purchase items outright from collectors, in which case the collector should expect to receive as little as 50% of the current quote price; perhaps even less. In this case, the dealer considers the secondary market transaction the same as a regular retail sale: he or she buys the item at about 50% of retail and then takes it into inventory. When it is sold, the proceeds cover overhead, inventory costs, and costs of doing business as well as profit.

A continuing trend among dealers is to specialize in the secondary market for just one or two lines. There are still a handful of dealers who are knowl-edgeable on a wide range of collectibles and are willing to buy and sell them. However, collectors may have to contact the manufacturer's customer service department or an organization such as Collectors' Information Bureau to locate a "specialist" who can sell their particular piece of artwork.

Secondary Market Action is Sought by Only a Few

Our dealer experts agree that the vast majority of collectors purchase their items with very little thought of secondary market potential. At the most, they look forward to showing off their "smart buys" to friends as they watch prices rise for their favorite collectibles.

Most secondary market buys, our experts say, are executed by collectors who are hoping to fill out a series or acquire an item of special significance that they were unable to purchase on the primary market.

Some sellers enjoy "trading up" to more expensive collectibles, and finance their new purchases by selling items that once were quite affordable — but now command high prices on the auction market. There are also a number of collectors who wish to sell certain items because of a lifestyle change, move to smaller quarters, or financial hardship. And sometimes those who inherit collections are not in a position to keep and display them.

Whatever a collector's reason for buying or selling on the secondary market, the keys to success are education, patience, rational thinking, and advice from the experts. That includes ready access to the resources of Collectors' Information Bureau. For answers to your secondary market questions, send a self-addressed, stamped envelope to the Collectors' Information Bureau at 2420 Burton S.E., Grand Rapids, Michigan 49546.

Insuring Your Collectibles
How to Establish Your Collection's Worth...and Protect Your Treasures Against Loss or Theft

Imagine returning from an evening on the town to discover that your home has been ransacked...your favorite artwork and collectibles stolen. The feelings of violation and fear would be difficult enough to deal with. But imagine your shock if you should find that your insurance policy did not cover the full value of your favorite works of art!

In a very short time, plates, figurines and other collectibles may double, triple or even soar in value to ten times their original prices or more. And collectors who started out to buy "just a few things to display here and there" may soon find themselves the proud owners of scores of pieces — worth many thousands of dollars.

So how does the intelligent collector protect those precious assets? Experts suggest a plan that combines prevention and risk management. Begin by doing all you can to make sure your home does not become a target for crime. Then find out how much each of your art pieces is worth, and work with an insurance specialist to develop a protection plan that fits your needs and budget.

Prevent Theft Through Home Preparedness

In today's society, electronic protection devices have become the "locks" of ultimate security. The first choice for any burglar is a home or site that has no electronic security system. There are many excellent companies now offering home systems that can be especially designed for your particular home and collection. These firms can be easily located by checking your local yellow pages under the "security" heading.

There are several points to consider when purchasing a security system. Some systems operate with batteries at the point of contact, and these batteries either need to be replaced on occasion or checked regularly by the security firm's employees. A system that relies primarily on batteries and constant maintenance by company employees may not be the most effective form of protection. The most effective systems ring into a central station where the local police are dispatched on a 24-hour basis.

While having a burglar alarm installed, it is usually wise to also connect a smoke/fire alarm to the system, thereby offering yourself further protection against another type of loss that could occur. In any case, shop around and compare systems before making your selection. Speak with other collectors that you respect and get their comments regarding systems they have purchased.

Your precautionary measures may well reap benefits on your insurance policy: such items as deadbolt locks, central alarms, smoke detectors and available fire extinguishers may result in valuable credits against the cost of your coverage.

How to Plan for Out-of-Town Travel

Russell J. Lindemann, Assistant Vice-President of Hilb, Rogal, and Hamilton Company of Grand Rapids, Michigan, offers his insurance clients a few simple tips that may help avoid break-ins during vacations or business trips. "If you're going away, take your most valuable items to someone else's house for safe keeping, or put them in a bank vault," Lindemann suggests. "You might place smaller and less fragile items in your safety deposit box.

"It's worth reminding people to leave some lights on timers when they go out of town," Lindemann continues. "I suggest one or two upstairs, one or two downstairs, and one in the kitchen. I vary their times a bit each day. I leave a radio on a timer, too. Mine goes on from about 11 p.m. to 3 a.m. If someone approaches the house and hears that sound from outside, they'll be less likely to try to enter.

"The less people who know you are away from home, the better," Lindemann counsels. "While some advisors will tell you to stop your mail and newspaper delivery, you never know who might overhear that order. I prefer to have a family member, trusted neighbor or close friend pick up the mail and newspaper each day while I'm gone." Lindemann has some suggestions for winter travelers, too. "Have someone shovel your driveway and a path up to the front walk. Or arrange to have someone pull up to your garage to make tracks. It's a dead giveaway that no one's home if your driveway is left unshoveled for days after a major snowstorm." The same goes for summertime lawn mowing if you'll be gone for more than a week.

Lindemann's associate, Kay Scoville, says it's a good idea to have someone go in and check on your home periodically while you are away. "Don't leave the storm door unlocked for them," Ms. Scoville says. "It's best to have as many locks and deterrents as possible. One idea is to leave your garage door down and give the garage door opener or key to the person who's checking your house. When they leave and put down the door, the house is locked up tight again."

Establishing the Value of Your Collectibles

While some collectors assume that their favorite works of art are automatically covered under the "contents" provisions of their homeowners or renters policies, Lindemann and Ms. Scoville warn that it's never safe to assume.

"The 'contents' amount is usually determined as a percentage of your home's value, but it can be increased. The percentage differs from company to company, but the majority are in the area of 50 to 70% of your home's replacement cost," Lindemann explains. In the case of a total loss, problems may arise if an individual owns a relatively modest home but has a large collection of valuable pieces — or pieces that have risen substantially in value.

"In addition, there's the question of irreplaceable, one-of-a-kind items," Lindemann continues. "How do you set a value on them? They need to

Insurance agent Thomas A. Mier from Universal Insurance Services, Inc., Grand Rapids, Michigan, explains the types of coverage available to collectors and the importance of adequately insuring valuable possessions.

be appraised, and scheduled individually on your insurance policy."

While the prices listed in books such as this *Collectibles Market Guide and Price Index* may be considered adequate documentation by many insurance firms, Lindemann emphasizes that especially rare, valuable or controversial pieces often may require individual appraisal.

What is an Appraiser, and How Do I Choose One?

Some collectors are unsure as to whether they need the services of an appraiser, and if so, how they should choose the best appraiser for their needs. To provide guidance in this important area, Collectors' Information Bureau solicited the advice of Emyl Jenkins, author of *Emyl Jenkins' Appraisal Book: Identifying, Understanding, and Valuing Your Treasures* (Crown Publishers). Ms. Jenkins' book is available for $24.95 in major bookstores or by writing her for an autographed copy at Emyl Jenkins Appraisals, P.O. Box 12465, Raleigh, NC 27605.

An appraiser is a person who determines the value of an item or items for insurance purposes, and can supply the necessary information for the settlement of damage claims. The professional appraiser is also the person who can determine the value of a collection at the time it is donated to a tax-exempt institution or charity.

While the *New York Times* estimates that there are an estimated 125,000 appraisers in the United States, it is up to the individual collector to evaluate an appraiser's qualifications. Ms. Jenkins offers this advice:

"The American Society of Appraisers is recognized as this country's only multidisciplinary appraisal testing designation society. Membership in the ASA is not necessarily proof of ability. It does mean, however, that the ASA member has submitted his appraisals for examination by his peers, has taken and passed a multisection examination on ethics, appraisal principals, and his specialized area, and is experienced.

"Because of the rigid requirements imposed on its members, the American Society of Appraisers is often referred to as the most prestigious of the appraisal organizations. The ASA and the International Society of Appraisers both have excellent educational programs conducted under college and university auspices. These two professional associations also grant their members different levels of professional proficiency as a result of successful course completion and/or testing. The Appraisers

Association of America is also widely recognized, and applicants must submit appraisals and meet AAA requirements before they are accepted as members.

"Locally, you may find personal property appraisers listed in the yellow pages, but if not, call your insurance agent, bank, attorney, or museum. A call to a college or university art department may be worthwhile. You can also check with antique shops, interior decorators, or auction houses. They may offer appraisal services or refer you to an independent appraiser."

According to Ms. Jenkins, the cost of appraisal services should be comparable to that of other professional services in your locale — attorney or accounting fees, for example. Hourly rates range from $35 to $150 per hour or $350 to $1,500 per day. Do not expect to be charged only for the time your appraiser spends with you. Appraisers must also charge for their research and appraisal preparation time. You will be wise to negotiate a contract spelling out prices and services before beginning to work with your appraiser.

Keep a Detailed Inventory of Your Holdings

Even items which do not call for individual appraisal should be carefully documented in your collectibles records. With some insurance policies, it may not be possible to receive reimbursement for the full value of your collection without a comprehensive list. Record the following basic information for each item:

- Manufacturer Name
- Edition Limit/Your Item's Number if Numbered
- Artist Name
- Your Cost
- Series Name
- Added Expenses (Shipping, Framing, Restoration, etc.)
- Item Name
- Special Markings (Artist's Signature, etc.)
- Year of Issue
- Secondary Market History (If Purchased on Secondary Market)
- Size/Dimensions
- Place of Purchase
- Location in Your Home (For Burglary or Loss)
- Date of Purchase
- Insurance Company/Policy or Rider Number

Of course, you will also keep any appraisal documents with your inventory list. Record each new item you buy at the time of purchase. Large index cards will handle the pertinent information, or you may prefer to invest in one of the published record books that may be available in your local bookstore.

The Importance of Video Documentation

Collectors should take advantage of today's video technology to provide a full-color, close-up record of all valuable possessions on tape. If you do not own a video camera, rent one for an afternoon and equip yourself with this essential "video documentation."

Begin with a general overview of the entire collection to provide a "feel" for how extensive it is, and how you normally display your pieces. Then tape a detailed close-up of each individual piece. Hold up each item so that the markings on base or backstamp can be read. Close-ups should offer special views of details and any printed wording on the items.

After you have finished with your video record, replay the film to check the quality and then rewind for storage with your written inventory in a site off-premises: perhaps in your safe deposit box. Make a copy of your video and written inventory so that another set can be kept at home.

Options and Choices for Collectibles Insurance

Once you have "burglar proofed" your home, established values for your collectibles, and documented your holdings, you are ready to make an informed decision about your fine arts insurance coverage. It is a good idea to get two or three different companies to quote you a price, since different insurance companies specialize in certain kinds of policies. Or talk with a multi-line firm like Hilb, Rogal, and Hamilton, where Russell J. Lindemann and other staff members do the legwork for you and present you with recommendations of the best company and policy for your needs.

There are several types of coverage available today: valuable articles coverage (VAC), homeowner's or renter's, a separate endorsement to an existing policy, an endorsement on a business policy, or a completely separate policy.

Once you have established your insurance coverage, you can breathe easy for a time. But don't

It is important to keep an accurate record of your collectible purchases. Both record books above provide space for photographs and pertinent information.

forget to consider the impact of new acquisitions: should they be appraised? Should they be listed individually on your fine arts rider? As Lindemann says, "You have to keep up. If you don't modify your policy and a loss occurs, you can't collect more than what's shown on the policy. And if something you own is going up in value, make sure you adjust the value shown for it in your policy at least every year or two."

Protecting one's collection may seem like an arduous task, but the time invested is well worth the rewards of peace of mind and proper coverage. And like many collectors, you may even find that you enjoy the process of documentation and valuation — as it reinforces the growing scope and value of your wonderful collection!

The Collectors' Information Bureau thanks Dean A. Genth of Miller's Gift Gallery, Eaton, Ohio, for his substantial contributions to this article.

C.I.B. Associate Members
Mattheyprint and Custom China Work Behind the Scenes to Produce Some of the World's Most Honored Collector Plates

The gleaming porcelain plates that you see in your favorite collectibles shop — or admire in ads and direct mailings — require months of skilled and devoted work to design and produce. And two firms whose outstanding efforts have contributed to many an award-winning plate are Mattheyprint Corporation, a decal maker, and Custom China Creations, a collector plate decorator.

Mattheyprint's work comes first: using the original artwork selected for a plate as the basis for the creation of perfectly faithful ceramic art transfers. Custom China uses such transfers in the decoration, firing and finishing of plates to beautifully reflect the artist's original. As this story unfolds, you will come to understand the intricacy and care which are necessary for the successful completion of this step-by-step process of art reproduction on porcelain.

A Decal Maker of International Stature

Mattheyprint Corporation is the United States sales office for ceramic decals printed at Matthey Transfers, England and Matthey Beyrand et Cie of Limoges, France. These two factories have long and respected histories for supplying ceramic decals to the world's finest names in tableware, glassware and collectible plates. Familiar brand names such as Royal Doulton, Wedgwood, Spode and Ainsley all are decorated with Matthey ceramic decals.

For the past fifteen years, the French firm of Matthey Beyrand et Cie has concentrated on the production of high-quality collectible plate decals and is now considered one of the premiere suppliers for the limited edition market. The Johnson Matthey Group, of which Matthey Transfers, Matthey Beyrand and Mattheyprint are parts, have made a commitment to quality and customer service on behalf of their over 7,000 worldwide employees.

One of the most knowledgeable of these employees, Norm D. Cote, serves as U.S. Sales Manager for Johnson Matthey. His expertise in the crafting of ceramic decals has led to his authorship of an authoritative description of the process, which is quoted liberally with his permission in the paragraphs to follow.

The Art of Decal Making Stage I: Planning

Norm Cote stresses the importance of pre-planning before any collector plate decal is produced. Indeed, as he says, "a ceramic decal is a complex art within itself; an amalgamation of artistry, printing and ceramics.

"Long before reproduction of the artwork is begun, even before a ceramic decal manufacturer is involved, the producer should have clearly outlined his goals: number of plates to be produced, size of the plate, and retail price." According to Cote, all of these factors help determine how the decal manufacturer will proceed.

Choosing the ceramic colors to match the artwork from previously printed color palette.

The Color Separation Process

Collector plate decals "are printed one color at a time," Cote explains, "using ceramic pigments to 'build' the final design. The printed image is held together by a covercoat or 'carrier'." This "carrier" becomes volatile when high-temperature firing takes place, leaving behind the ceramic colors, which fuse into the glaze of the plate.

Some ceramic decals are printed in a four-color process, like that used in commercial printing. In this case, the four basic "process" colors of black, magenta (red), yellow and cyan (blue) are used in combination to create all other necessary colors. This process does not allow for the exact reproduction of every color in an artist's palette or in nature, however. Thus many producers elect to use "picked" colors — sometimes twenty or more for an individual transfer.

As Cote tells us, "We have never been able to influence the DeGrazias, Rockwells and Hibels of the world to create their fine art in just the four primary colors. Their subtle nuances of color are at the same time an integral part of their attraction and the basis for much time consumption in their reproduction.

"The color separation expert must predetermine, for instance, what percentage of red and yellow will faithfully capture the facial tones of a Rockwell painting. Too much red will give a sunburned appearance; too much yellow, and 'jaundice' will be the diagnosis!"

Reproduction artist "separating" colors prior to printing.

How Collector Plate Decals are Printed

A familiar tale from Norm Cote helps explain the challenges that beset the printer of collector plate decals. "The house needs a fresh coat of paint. A quick trip to the hardware store and we're ready. Little by little, stroke by stroke, a new gleaming finish is applied. But — a breeze springs up and our still tacky finish is covered with airborne particles of dust and grit, not to mention a few members of the insect world. A disappointing result at best.

"However, it is precisely this basic phenomenon which is an integral part of the printing of a ceramic decal for a collectible plate. Basically, the decal manufacturer substitutes clear varnish for the house paint and ceramic color (in powder form) for the airborne dust and grit. In the controlled atmosphere of a pressroom, the two are combined. The dry ceramic dust adheres itself to the clear, wet varnish in specific areas designated by the color separa-

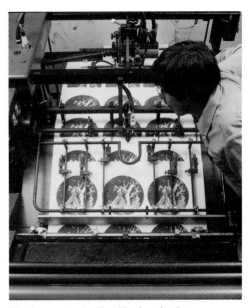

Nearly completed collectible plate decals in production.

tion. This two-step process, the laying on of a clear varnish on each sheet and the 'dusting' of ceramic color is collectively referred to as the printing stage of lithographic ceramic decal manufacture."

The paper used for the making of a ceramic decal is like ordinary paper in that it originates from wood fiber. But unlike the paper in this book, decal paper has a smooth, glossy coating on one side only. The coating disintegrates when dipped in water, so that the decal can slide off the paper and onto a plate.

Norm Cote cautions that the actual printing process for decals is much more complex than a trip to the neighborhood speedy printer. "Because of the special varnish used and its drying characteristics, only one color can be printed per day." That means that a twenty-five color decal would require five full working weeks to complete.

The Decals Arrive at Custom China

Once Matthey's richly colored, top-quality decals are completed, finally inspected, packaged and ready for shipment to the decorator, a firm like Custom China Creations takes center stage in the plate production process. In business for a dozen years, Custom China is capably run by its president, Bob Perkins — an expert with twenty-five years' experience in the field of ceramics.

Perkins holds a master's degree in ceramic engineering, and he worked in ceramics research before joining the famed Franciscan dinnerware firm some years ago. He ran the fine china production department at Gorham, Inc. for five years before opening the California-based Custom China Creations in 1979.

Perkins attributes his firm's success to the level of expertise his staff members bring to their work. "Each of our employees is hand-picked, and many of them have ten years' experience or more," Perkins explains.

When Custom China begins work on an edition of plates, the first step — in addition to the selection of appropriate ceramic ware and added decorations like gold banding — is the "proofing" of the plate. This process requires the concentration not only of decal maker and decorator, but of artist and producer. All four parties are equally concerned that the resulting "proof plate" offers the best possible image of the artist's original.

In "proofing," the decal maker provides a decorator like Custom China with a sample of the decals it has produced, before the full edition of decals is printed. Then Custom China uses the decals to decorate and fire some border or rim adornments. It is Custom China's job to determine the correct firing temperature and timing, in collaboration with the decal maker. According to Bob Perkins, sometimes experimentation is necessary to "fine tune" the firing process. And in some cases, the fired plates may show that the colors of the decals need adjustment before the full edition is printed.

Final, decal by decal, inspection prior to shipment to the decorator.

How Plates are Decorated and Fired at Custom China

With 40,000 square feet of production space available, Custom China is already considered a "state of the art" facility for collector plate decorating and firing. Yet Bob Perkins is committed to staying "ahead of the times." He has a 60,000 square foot facility on the drawing board, for completion within the next few years. "The equipment will be all-new," Perkins says. "We will be able to implement automated gold banding equipment,

and we'll use newest continuous belt kiln design, called a 'lehr'."

Yet even with his firm's up-to-date equipment in place, Perkins understands full well that it is the human touch that sets Custom China apart. Each plate that is decorated and fired in this facility is monitored from beginning to end by highly trained, quality-conscious artisans.

The creation of a single collector plate requires a multi-step process that begins with inspection of each decal and plate blank. For many firms, Custom China is entrusted with the selection and purchase of blank plates in sizes ranging from a "micro mini" of 1" in diameter to a dramatic, 16" round piece.

"When the plate blanks arrive here," Bob Perkins tells us, "we thoroughly inspect them for warpage, pinholes, black spots and edge quality. We also 'dry spot' the decals, an inspection process that ensures that each has outstanding quality of registration and uniformity of color, with no stray color deposits.

"After eliminating blanks and decals that are not completely perfect, we decorate a small number of plates for a test firing. We use only de-ionized water in the decoration process, to avoid any sodium or calcium deposits that might mar the finished plates. When the test firing is approved, we implement the production run.

"As each plate is decorated and hand-numbered, it is re-inspected to ensure that it has no visible flaws of any kind. After each plate is numbered, it is allowed to dry for a full twenty-four hours before firing," Perkins explains.

The kilns used for collector plate firing allow each plate to be slowly and uniformly heated to the temperature level necessary to allow the ceramic colors to fuse forever to the porcelain. They come out of the kiln already cooled, and then are taken to a final inspection center.

"At the time of this final inspection," Bob Perkins relates, "each plate is supplied with its own Certificate of Authenticity, numbered to match the number on its backstamp. Then the plates are packaged along with any literature the producer or marketer has supplied. Of course, all of our packaging is tested for its protective qualities and safety for transportation via United Parcel Service and the U.S. Postal Service."

Once a plate leaves the care of Custom China, it may be on its way initially to a retail store or dealer, or to the warehouse of a direct mail marketer. In any event, each plate is created in the hope that it will ultimately reside in the care of an individual collector who appreciates its handsome art…and its intricate production process.

The Production Process
How Figurines Are Made

Leaf through the pages of this book and you will view an endless variety of handsome collectibles that fall into the broad categories of "figurines." The elegant, hand-painted porcelains of Lenox and Kaiser...the shimmering crystal birds and animals of Swarovski...the appealing wood carvings of ANRI...the charming cottages of John Hine, Lilliput Lane, and Department 56.

Some figurines are crafted using age-old processes like the Goebel Miniatures' lost wax method, while others utilize state-of-the-art techniques like porcelain cold casting. Some pieces are left unadorned so that the innate beauty of polished bronze or pristine white bisque porcelain may be admired in all its glory. Others are painted in myriad individual colors...underglazed...overglazed...or burnished.

When collectors come to understand the complexity and care invested in even the simplest limited edition figurines, their enjoyment and appreciation may be greatly heightened. What's more, such knowledge enables collectors to evaluate possible purchases based upon the value of their materials and the intricacy of their design and production, as well as the appeal of their subject matter. This article provides a brief introduction to several of the step-by-step processes that bring today's figurines alive in three dimensions.

The Classic Limited Edition Porcelain Figurine

The limited edition figurine is a Twentieth Century invention: in the 1930s, Royal Worcester and its master artist, Dorothy Doughty, first perfected a method for casting exact replicas from an original, master sculpture. A very similar process still is used today by fine porcelain studios, as exemplified by this step-by-step technique employed at the American studios of Lenox Collections.

First, an artist creates an original sculpture, from which intricate molds are made. A phenomenal number of mold-parts are required for each porcelain: a single, three and one-half inch bird sculpture might require thirty-eight parts! While using so many individual mold parts is costly, Lenox considers it well worthwhile to produce lifelike poses and deeper detailing.

Next, liquid porcelain "slip" is poured into each mold. The formula of the porcelain slip will be varied to meet specific artist requirements for color and detail. Lenox, like most fine porcelain studios, limits the "lifetime use" of each mold. Thus, the sculptured detail stays especially crisp and sharp.

The resulting fragile castings, called "greenware," must be hand-assembled and propped for firing. If this is not done correctly, the sculpture

#1 — The making of a classic Royal Doulton Character Jug begins as liquid slip is poured into a mold. The porous mold absorbs the moisture from the china "slip" and leaves a coating of china in the form of the character jug inside.

#2 — Excess slip is poured away after approximately twenty minutes.

#3 — The mold is carefully opened to reveal a character jug inside.

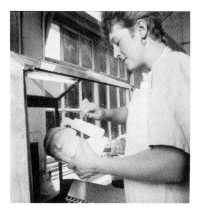  

#4 — The handle of "The Golfer," modeled to portray a bag of golf clubs, is attached to the main body of the piece.

#5 and #6 — After drying, the jug is brushed and smoothed to remove any mold marks or rough edges of china.

will "slump" in the kiln and compromise the desired effect. Craftsmen at Lenox reject even minor "slumps" to ensure the artistic integrity of each sculpture.

A typical Lenox sculpture is fired in the kiln four separate times. The first firing takes place at temperatures as high as 1330 degrees Centigrade, and can last as long as thirteen to twenty-four hours.

From the fiery tips of an autumn leaf to the blush of a shy young maiden, details come to life only if painted to perfection. Lenox-trained artisans take extra care in hand-painting every sculpture, often using an unusually rich palette of colors. Each hand-painted work then is kiln-fired to fuse the ceramic colors to the porcelain.

A Time-Consuming Creative Process

While the Lenox process described above offers an overview of porcelain craftsmanship, some large and complex porcelain works may require many more steps — and much more time — for completion. As an example, WACO's "The Grand Carousel" consumed more than two years of research and development time and an investment of over $1,000,000 before its completion. In addition to the carousel itself, this sculptural work also includes a music box.

Other sculptures — notably those of Boehm and Royal Worcester — may combine porcelain with another sculptural medium such as burnished bronze. In these cases, delicate floral petals are cast in porcelain and fashioned into flowers by hand; then joined to stems and leaves of bronze which allow for durability as well as incredible detail work.

LEGENDS has gained fame and praise for its dynamic works of art — often on Western themes — which combine two or more precious metals for a rich and dramatic sculptural effect. Portions in bronze, silver, or other metals are cast individually, then joined together, adding dimension and beauty to the finished figurine.

An Up-and-Coming Art Form: Cold-Cast Porcelain

Renowned figurine makers including Border Fine Arts and Duncan Royale employ a fine art process called cold-casting. The formula for cold-casting may call for chips or dust of bronze, wood, or — most often — porcelain, combined with resin. The advantages of cold-casting include the cost savings of avoiding kiln firing, and the remarkable detail work that is possible when a figurine is cast in resin-based materials. This narrative describes the step-by-step process that takes place at the Border Fine Arts Studios to make popular figurines, such as those of Lowell Davis for Schmid.

Like the classic porcelain crafting process, each cold-cast porcelain figurine begins with an original sculpture, most often created in modeling wax. Next, a special mold-making silicone compound is carefully applied over the wax original to produce the master mold. There must be no mistakes during this operation, as the original may be lost and with it scores or even hundreds of hours of work.

Next, a metal composition casting is poured, and the resulting piece is used as a production master. The master is reworked with engraving tools to ensure that every detail is sharp and crisp. Then production molds and cases are made from this master, and injected with a liquid "slip" combining the resin and porcelain dust. A chemical reaction takes place under pressure, resulting in a white, porcelain-like casting that offers a faithful rendering of the sculptor's original.

These "whiteware" castings then are removed from their molds and set aside to cure. The castings are inspected for quality, and any which are not absolutely perfect are destroyed.

In a process called "fettling," a team of skilled artisans prepares the raw, white castings for painting. Seams on the whiteware are removed with delicate dentistry drills, and sculptures with multiple parts are assembled in the fettling department. Another quality control inspection precedes the careful process of hand-painting.

In many cases, handsome wooden bases are added to the finished pieces, which are then enhanced by felt bottoms that protect the furniture in collectors' homes.

Mold-Making is the Key to a Successful Cottage

As collectible cottages gain more and more admirers each year, there is growing interest in the production process for these charming miniature homes, shops and public buildings. Here is an overview of the making of one of the much-loved David Winter cottages for John Hine Limited.

The most difficult and fundamental part of the production work is the making of the molds for each original cottage. Indeed, the sole purpose of every craftsperson who works on the cottages is to produce exact replicas of David Winter's own intricately modeled pieces. This stage requires scrupulous care, since each cottage emerges from one single mold, which must capture every nuance of detail.

The successful mold is passed to the casters who use it to produce a perfect cast in a special material called Crystacal. Crystacal is a form of natural gypsum which is filtered, dried and ground to a powder. When added to water, it becomes an excellent, perfectly pure casting material.

Each minute feature inside the mold must be fingered carefully to ensure that none of the finer

#7 — Jug being placed onto a kiln car which will transport it through a tunnel kiln for its first firing. This firing process takes 18 hours at 1260 degrees C.

#8 — Character jugs on cart at entrance of the kiln.

#9 — The Royal Doulton backstamp is applied to the bottom of the jug.

#10 — Each jug is carefully hand-painted. Jugs are painted on the biscuit body before glazing to achieve a stronger, more character-like look or style of decoration.

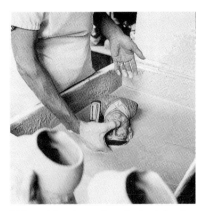

#11 — After decoration, the jug is hand dipped in a vat of glaze and then will be fired in the kiln a final time.

details is missed. The exact position of everything inside the mold is essential, and thus the craftspeople who carry out this process must employ the greatest possible degree of concentration.

Next the mold is removed from the cast slowly and deliberately, to ensure that the model itself is not damaged. If the emerging cast piece is anything less than perfect, it is destroyed.

After the cast has been removed from the mold, "flashes" of Crystacal are still attached to it. These small pieces of excess material are delicately "fettled" away and the base is made smooth and even.

At this stage, the cast is set, but not yet completely dry. To allow the cottage to reach the correct consistency for the next process, it is "rested" in a temperature controlled room in conditions of suitable humidity. A sealing solution of shellac and white polish is used to coat the models next; this acts as an undercoat for the painting. Then when the sealing solution has dried fully, the unpainted models are delivered to the homes of John Hine Limited's skilled team of painters.

Those selected as painters are taught the delicate skill of staining the cottages in a manner which highlights the artistry and detailing of David Winter's work. The subtle colors, and the special techniques used by the painters, emphasize the realism of Winter's miniature cottages. A final inspection, the addition of felt on each cottage base, and careful packaging complete the creation of a handsome new collectible cottage.

ANRI Wood Carvings Carry on the European Tradition

Also included in the category of figurines are the wonderful wood carvings of Italy's ANRI Workshops, which are presented in the United States by Schmid. Each wood carving begins with the unblemished wood of an Austrian Alpine maple tree, which is prepared with care and hand-carved by a skilled craftsperson.

Once a rough cut for carving is prepared on a lathe, the sculptor uses progressively smaller and finer tools to gradually work toward an extremely fine detailed carving. After many hours of painstaking carving, ANRI figures arrive in the hands of the painters. Special, transparent oil colors are produced for ANRI in Italy, while stains for the sculptures are produced in Germany.

The Sparkling Story of Crystal Sculpture

Often today, the term "crystal" is used loosely to describe any fine glass. But the regulations of the European Economic Community (EEC) make the legal definition of this substance very specific — indeed, "crystal clear." In order to be sold as Full Lead Crystal, a glass product must be made with at least 30% lead. Crystal that contains 30% lead or more has the potential for incredible brilliance and maximum refraction when the crystal stones are cut and polished.

While some of us think of handsome dinner goblets when we hear the word "crystal," today this coveted substance is used to make a menagerie of animals, birds and other handsome, sculptural collectibles by Swarovski America.

Whether you prefer your three-dimensional collectibles in fine porcelain, cold-cast porcelain, precious metal, wood or crystal, today's art studios offer you a wide variety of elegant figurines. In all price ranges…all sizes…and every degree of complexity, figurines make a superb addition to any home. And when you understand the careful process by which they are created, your enjoyment of these works of sculptural art increases all the more!

#12 — Golfer character jugs being removed from the kiln.

#13 — Each jug is carefully inspected to ensure that it meets quality control before it is allowed to leave the factory.

The Finished Product

"When Coffee Never Tasted So Good" by Lowell Davis from Schmid

Club ANRI's "Twenty Years of Love" by Juan Ferrandiz

"The Grand Carousel" from WACO Products Corporation

"Squires Hall" from John Hine Studios

Lenox Collections' "Polar Bear"

Duncan Royale's "May" from the Calendar Secrets collection

Flambro Imports' "65th Birthday Commemorative"

LEGENDS' "Pursued" by C.A. Pardell

"Hippopotamus," "Elephant" and "Rhinoceros" from
Swarovski America

Travel for Collectors
Broaden Your Knowledge of Collecting by Visiting Museums and Touring Collectible Production Facilities

Collectors who vacation in the United States, Canada and abroad are invited to browse through this chapter to discover the locations of exciting collectible tours and museums offered by manufacturers and other firms.

Attend a barbecue. Participate in an auction. Tour your favorite collectible factory and enjoy their step-by-step production process. The opportunities are endless. Collectors who take the opportunity to experience their hobby first-hand, are certain to gain a deeper appreciation of their artwork and how it was crafted.

United States Museums and Tours

AMERICAN MUSEUM OF WILDLIFE ART
P.O. Box 26
3303 North Service Drive
Red Wing, MN 55066
612/388-0755

Open Monday-Saturday, 10 A.M.-5 P.M. Sunday, Noon-4 P.M. Closed all major holidays.

Located in Red Wing, Minnesota, fifty-five miles southeast of St. Paul and Minneapolis on U.S. 61.

Admission free, donations welcome, nature shoppe.

It is a non-profit organization established to further interest in wildlife art — collecting, presenting, honoring and preserving art in this field. The museum has five rotating exhibits yearly.

ANNALEE DOLL MUSEUM
P.O. Box 708
Meredith, NH 03253
800/433-6557

The factory is open only during the Barbecue & Auction weekend to the public. Tour hours are 8 A.M.-4 P.M. both days.

Located at the end of Reservoir Road and Hemlock Drive in Meredith, New Hampshire.

The Barbecue & Auction event includes two auctions, tours of the factory, special offers to attendees, live music, food and a 'meet-the-artist' party.

Tickets are $15.00 for each Doll Society member, $15.00 for first guest and $20.00 for each additional guest thereafter.

Call for date of this wonderful event.

BABYLAND GENERAL® HOSPITAL
19 Underwood St.
Cleveland, GA 30528
404/865-2171

Hospital hours are Monday thru Saturday, 9 A.M.-5 P.M. and Sunday, 1-5 P.M.

Admission is free.

Visitors will see where the Magic Crystal Tree grows within early 1900s medical clinic and Licensed Patch Nurses performing deliveries of original Cabbage Patch Kids®. The gift shop is open during tour hours and guided tours are available. Cabbage Patch Kids are available for adoption at the hospital as well as everything needed to care for them at the gift shop.

Ready to be "adopted" just minutes after birth, original Cabbage Patch Kids® are "delivered" daily from the Mother Cabbages near the Magic Crystal Tree at Babyland General® Hospital in Cleveland, Ga. A Licensed Patch Nurse proudly presents a brand new baby to enchanted visitors who have witnessed the entire birth!

MARTY BELL GALLERY
9424 Eton Avenue
Chatsworth, CA 91311
800/637-4537

The Gallery is open on Mondays only from 9 A.M. to 5 P.M.

Reservations are required by calling. The tour is limited to members of the *Marty Bell Collector's Society*.

The guided tour is approximately one hour. Visitors will see Marty Bell's publishing facility including Marty's originals' gallery. The originals' gallery features many original oil paintings never seen by the general public.

BELL HAVEN
c/o Iva Mae Long
R.D. #4 Box 54
Tarentum, PA 15084
412/265-2872

Tours are by appointment only.

Located on one acre of wooded grounds with bells located inside and out of the workshop.

Admission is $4.00.

Collectors will marvel at the 30,000 bells on display that have been gathered through the years beginning in the late 1950s.

BELLINGRATH GARDENS AND HOME/ BOEHM GALLERY
12401 Bellingrath Garden Rd.
Theodore, AL 36582
205/973-2217

Open daily 7 A.M.-dusk.

Located twenty miles southwest of Mobile off Interstate 10, Exit 15A to Theodore.

Reservations recommended for group tours and for groups of twenty or more.

Admission for the Garden is $5.00 adults, children 6-11 $2.50. Under 6 free. Home tour is $6.25 (except babes in arms). Boehm Gallery included in gardens.

Boehm Gallery has the largest public display of Boehm porcelains in the world. Over 225 porcelains are exhibited in lighted cases behind glass. The Bellingrath Home has a large collection of porcelains, crystal, silver, paintings and furniture from around the world. Hostesses conduct tours of the homes. The Bellingrath Gardens consist of sixty-five acres which include a bird sanctuary and chapel. The gardens are planned so as to be in bloom year-round.

Gift shop opens at 7 A.M. Cafeteria serves breakfast and lunch from 7 A.M.-3 P.M.

THE BRADFORD MUSEUM OF COLLECTOR'S PLATES
9333 Milwaukee Avenue
Niles, IL 60648
708/966-2770

Located in the Chicago suburb of Niles, Illinois.

The Bradford Museum of Collector's Plates is the world's largest permanent exhibit of limited edition collector's plates.

The museum's collection contains porcelain, china, silver and wood plates which were produced by over seventy makers from more than sixteen countries.

In the center of the museum is The Bradford Exchange Trading Floor where brokers help clients buy and sell plates over the telephone. The trading floor is the heart of the dynamic international collector's plate market in North America, Europe and Australia.

Since its opening in 1978, the museum has attracted more than 100,000 visitors from all fifty states and nine foreign countries.

The museum is currently under renovation and is slated to open in the fall of 1991. For more information on tour hours and admission prices, contact the museum.

THE BYERS' CHOICE MUSEUM
Wayside Country Store
1015 Boston Post Road Rt. 20
Marlborough, MA 01752
508/481-3458

Open seven days a week from 10 A.M.-5 P.M.

Located at the famous Wayside Country Store on the Marlborough/Sudbury Massachusetts line.

The museum houses many old and rare collectible Byers Choice Carolers. Many of them are pieces that collectors have never seen.

The historical Wayside Country Store was restored and operated by Henry Ford in 1929. The Wayside Country Store has fourteen specialty shops. Nearby is the very famous Longfellow's "Wayside Inn," The Little Red School House that the poem "Mary Had a Little Lamb" was written about. The Martha/Mary Chapel, a very picturesque non-denominational chapel where hundreds of weddings are performed each year is also close by. Both the chapel and the beautiful Stone Grist Mill were built by Heny Ford. It is a very picturesque New England setting.

There is no admission fee.

CIRCUS WORLD MUSEUM
426 Water St.
Baraboo, WI 53913
608/356-8341
608/356-0800 — seasonal information line

Museum exhibit buildings and grounds are open 9 A.M.-6 P.M. early May thru mid-September except late July through late August when the grounds are open until 10 P.M. The grounds include live shows.

Irvin Field Exhibit Hall and Visitor Center open year round. Located in south central Wisconsin, 12 miles from the Wisconsin Dells in Baraboo.

Admission charge is $8.95 for adults, seniors $7.95, children 3-12 $5.50 and under 3 free. Includes all shows, exhibits and demonstrations.

The world's largest facility devoted to the circus, it is located on the site of the Ringling Brothers Circus original winterquarters (1884-1918). The world's largest repository of circus antiques, artifacts and information is recognized by the American Association of Museums and is a National Historic Site. (Collectors of Flambro's Emmett Kelly, Jr. collectibles would find this museum especially interesting.)

LOWELL DAVIS' RED OAK II
Rt. 1
Carthage, MO 64836
417/358-1943

Tour hours are 10 A.M.-6 P.M., Monday-Saturday.

Admission is free for the self-guided tour.

The tour includes buildings from the 1930s era on forty acres of land. Buildings that will be open to visitors are a school house, general store, gas station, church, blacksmith shop, saw mill and the reception center which includes original art works by Lowell Davis. The Belle Starr Museum is also in the area and admission is $1.00.

FAVELL MUSEUM OF WESTERN ART AND INDIAN ARTIFACTS
125 West Main Street
Klamath Falls, OR 97601
503/882-9996

Monday-Saturday, 9:30-5:30, closed on Sundays.

Admission: $4 adults, $3 seniors, $1 children 6-16.

The museum overlooks the outlet of the largest natural lake in Oregon and its 17,000 square feet of display space is laid out like the spokes of a wagon wheel. Includes works by renowned western artists such as Donald Polland, John Clymer, Joe Beeler, Frank McCarthy, and Mort Kunstler, as well as more than eighty collections of artifacts, including miniature firearms. Gift shop and art gallery.

FENTON ART GLASS COMPANY
420 Caroline Avenue
Willaimstown, WV 26187
304/375-7772

Fenton Art Glass Company offers a free forty minute factory tour.

The factory tour runs Monday-Friday, beginning at 8:30 A.M. and the last leaving at 2:30 P.M. The factory is closed on national holidays and during an annual two week vacation always around the first two weeks of July.

Located in Williamstown, West Virginia, just across the Ohio River from Marietta, Ohio. The factory is easily reached by Interstate I-77, Exit 185, from West Virginia State Routes 2, 14, and US Route 50.

No reservations necessary for groups under 20; highly recommended for more than 20.

Admission free.

Tour of plant allows you to watch highly skilled craftsmen create handmade glass from molten state to finished product. Majority of factory tour handicap accessible.

The museum craftshop hours are: September-May, Monday-Saturday, 8 A.M.-5 P.M., except Tuesday and Thursday, open till 8 P.M.; Sunday 12 P.M.-5 P.M. June-August, Monday-Friday, 8 A.M.-8 P.M.; Saturday, 8 A.M.-5 P.M.; Sunday 12 P.M.-5 P.M.

The museum gift shop is closed only on Easter, Christmas, Thanksgiving and New Years Day.

Admission charges are $1 adults, 50 cents children 10-16, under 10 free and a 20% discount for groups of 20 or more.

The museum offers examples of Ohio Valley glass with major emphasis on Fenton glass made 1905-1955. Representative glass of other Ohio Valley companies is displayed along with items of historical interest. A thirty-minute movie on the making of Fenton Glass is shown at regular times throughout the day.

FJ DESIGNS CATS MEOW FACTORY
2163 Great Trails Drive
Wooster, OH 44691
216/264-1377

Tours at 10 A.M. and 1 P.M., Monday-Friday.

Admission is free. Reservations required with groups of more than six persons. No bus tours are available.

The tour is 45 minutes long and begins in the lobby area. In the lobby are displays of all retired and new products from FJ Designs, beginning in 1982. During the tour through the factory, the production processes of five different departments will be observed. These processes include sanding, spray painting, screen printing, and the finishing of the Cats Meow *Village* pieces.

FRANKLIN MINT MUSEUM
Franklin Center, PA 19091
215/459-6168

Closed Monday. Open Tuesday-Saturday 9:30 A.M.-4:30 P.M., Sunday 1:00 P.M.-4:30 P.M.
No reservations required.
Free admission.

The Franklin Mint Museum houses original masterpieces by such world-famous American artists as Andrew Wyeth and Norman Rockwell, as well as re-creations of works commissioned by the National Wildlife Federation, the Royal Shakespeare Theatre, the Louvre and The White House. You'll also see the finest works created by the world-famous artists of The Franklin Mint Studio. Extraordinary sculptures in porcelain, crystal, pewter and bronze. Award-winning collector dolls. Die-cast automotive classics. Uniquely designed and minted coins. Philatelics of historic significance. Handicap facilities provided. Special events, gallery store, free parking.

FRANKOMA POTTERY TOUR
P.O. Box 789
2400 Frankoma Road
Sapulpa, OK 74067
800/331-3650 or 918/224-5511

The gift shop is open 8 A.M.-6 P.M., Monday-Saturday, and 12:30-5 P.M. on Sunday. Tours begin at 9 A.M. until 3:15 P.M., Monday-Friday.

Admission is free. Reservations are highly recommended for large groups to ensure that not too many groups arrive at one time. Tours are every thirty minutes.

Located four miles southwest of Tulsa on Frankoma Road in Sapulpa, Oklahoma.

A very interesting tour for young and old of the pottery factory. On exhibit are 275 pieces of pottery made in thirteen colors, plus gift items. Frankoma has been producing fine pottery for fifty-eight years.

GALLERY IN THE SUN
6300 N. Swan Road
Tucson, AZ 85718
602/299-9191

Open seven days a week, 10 A.M.-4 P.M.

No admission charge.
Reservations needed for free guided tours.

Exhibits in this all-adobe museum include thirteen rooms of the works of Ted DeGrazia. Two of the rooms are rotated during the year, one being seasonal. Exhibits cover all types of DeGrazia sculptures and paintings, including his first painting, which he painted at the age of 16.

At Easter you can see The Way of The Cross which is DeGrazia's interpretations of the Fifteen Stations of The Cross. A series of Madonnas and angels are on display at Christmas time along with celebrating the Fiesta of Guadalupe. The museum closes promptly at 4 P.M. in keeping with DeGrazia's policy when he was alive. A gift shop is also open during tour hours.

GOEBEL MINIATURES STUDIOS/FACTORY
4820 Adohr Lane
Camarillo, CA 93012
805/484-4351

All tours must be booked in advance. Call the studio to make arrangements. The most common time for tours is Thursdays at 10 A.M.

No admission is charged.

Visitors will see a brief film about the production of the miniature figurines and then walk through the studios/factory to see close-up the developmental and decorative processes. The tour takes approximately one hour.

Goebel Miniature figures receive a priming coat of paint and are inspected for bubbles and mold marks in the grinding room before they go into the decorating studios.

SONJA HARTMANN ORIGINALS DOLL STUDIO
1230 Pottstown Pike
Glenmoore, PA 19343
215/458-1120

The studio is open 9 A.M.-5 P.M., Monday-Friday.

Tours are by appointment only. Bus groups are welcome.

Visitors will see the production of porcelain and vinyl dolls from the pouring of porcelain into the molds to the dressing and hair styling of the charming dolls.

Admission is free.

HIBEL MUSEUM OF ART
150 Royal Poinciana Plaza
Palm Beach, FL 33480
407/833-6870

Tours are Tuesday-Saturday, 10 A.M.-5 P.M.; Sunday, 1-5 P.M.

Admission is free. Reservations are requested for groups of ten or more. Bus tours are invited.

The museum opened in January 1977, as a tribute to artist Edna Hibel by the late Ethelbelle and Clayton B. Craig.

The Hibel Museum of Art has an extensive collection of Edna Hibel oil paintings, drawings, lithographs, porcelain collectables and dolls. Visitors will see antique snuff bottles, dolls and paperweight collection. The museum has a collection of rare art books and antique Oriental, English and Italian furniture.

The museum shop is open during tour hours.

JERRI DOLL'S COLLECTION ROOM
Dolls by Jerri Factory
651 Anderson St.
Charlotte, NC 28205
704/333-3211

The factory is open 9 A.M.-4 P.M., Monday-Friday.

No admission is charged. Tours are by appointment only and group size is limited to twenty visitors.

Visitors will see the showroom with a complete collection of every Jerri doll, plate, ornament, figurine created by Jerri since 1976. The steps in creating a Jerri doll can be seen on the tour, which includes the creative beginnings to shipping of the product from the factory.

LAWTONS' WORKSHOP
548 North First St.
Turlock, CA 95380
209/632-3655

Tours are by special arrangement to groups only. No admission charge.

Guests are treated to a step-by-step demonstration of Lawtons' actual doll production. Guests will see the process from the first pour of porcelain slip to the final inspection and packaging.

Lawtons provides a fascinating tour of its doll company to interested groups, including school tours.

LLADRO MUSEUM AND GALLERIES
43 West 57th Street
New York, NY 10019
212/838-9341

Open Tuesday-Saturday 10 A.M.-5:30 P.M. Reservations required for large groups. Free Admission.

The museum houses the largest collection of retired Lladro porcelains. Display features appoximately 2,500 pieces, and museum occupies three floors of the building.

The Lladro Art Gallery on the sixth floor is dedicated to inroducing the works of contemporary Spanish art to people in the United States.

LEE MIDDLETON ORIGINAL DOLLS
1301 Washington Boulevard
Belpre, Ohio 45714
800/233-7479

There is no charge for tours of the factory.

Lee Middleton Original Doll Company opens its doors to countless visitors from around the world. A larger-than-life doll house in every way, Lee's new manufacturing facility is discreetly hidden behind a beautiful pastel "gingerbread" facade which fronts her 37,000 square foot state-of-the-art production plant. Each tour provides a clear understanding of the creative process behind Lee's porcelain and vinyl collectible dolls. Visitors will see the mixing and pouring of liquid porcelain, the vinyl molding and curing process and the hand-painting of each doll's face.

The company schedules tours seven times daily, Monday-Friday, 9 A.M.-3 P.M., and is always pleased to host large group tours at requested times with adequate advance notice.

The Middleton Doll Company tour includes an opportunity to see how liquid porcelain is carefully poured into a plastic mold. To preserve the detail required in Lee's fine porcelain dolls, the plaster mold is destroyed after only a few pourings and replaced with a fresh mold.

PRECIOUS MOMENTS CHAPEL & VISITORS CENTER
P.O. Box 802
Carthage, MO 64836
800/543-7975

No admission fee. Free Guided Tours.

Reservations requested for large groups of fifteen or more. Please call for more information.

The chapel is open daily at 9 A.M., Monday-Sunday.

In a quiet setting, just outside the Victorian town of Carthage, Missouri stands the realization of a dream that was born in the heart of one of America's most famous artists, Sam Butcher.

Sam Butcher began the preliminary sketches of his dream four years ago on a flight to Asia. One finds the Precious Moments Chapel, a gallery of reverence nestled among the dogwood in the beautiful meadows of the Ozarks.

The fifteen stained glass windows are among the most exquisite treasures in the Chapel. The windows, with some containing over 1,200 individually cut pieces of glass, were painstakingly leaded by the artist's family.

The fifty-four murals, covering a total of almost five thousand square feet, are perhaps the most important works of Sam's life. Thirty-five feet above the marble floor, angels wing their way across a twenty-six hundred square foot ceiling as they celebrate the victory of our saviour's resurrection.

REED & BARTON FACTORY
144 W. Britannia St.
Taunton, MA 02780
800/822-1824, X308

Tours are by appointment only. The factory is open Monday-Friday, 8 A.M.-2 P.M. Located in scenic New England, the Reed & Barton factory is over 160 years old and is listed on the National Register of historic places.

See how Reed & Barton flatware is hand-crafted during a forty-five minute guided tour. Visitors will see the artists create from start to finish — transferring raw materials into elegant flatware.

Admission for the tour is free.

The Reed & Barton factory tour includes a look at the die-cutting operation.

NORMAN ROCKWELL CENTER/ FRANCES HOOK MUSEUM
315 Elizabeth Street
P.O. Box 91
Mishicot, WI 54228
414/755-4014

Monday through Saturday, 10 A.M.-4 P.M., Sunday 1-4 P.M., evenings by appointment.

Located in the Old School in the Village of Mishicot, Wisconsin.

Reservations requested for groups. (Contact Carol Anderson)

One of the largest Norman Rockwell collections in the world, free slide shows, shop displays of art, limited edition prints and collectibles. The Frances Hook Museum/Art Gallery features her limited edition issues and sponsors an annual Frances Hook Celebration in June, complete with Frances Hook Look-Alike Contest.

NORMAN ROCKWELL MUSEUM
601 Walnut Street
Philadelphia, PA 19106
215/922-4345

Open Monday-Saturday, 10 A.M.-4 P.M. and 11 A.M.-4 P.M. on Sunday.

Open everyday of the year except Christmas, New Year's, Thanksgiving and Easter.

Located 601 Walnut Street, lower level.

Reservations necessary for groups of 10 or more. Admission charge: adults, $2.00, seniors over 62 and AAA members, $1.50, children 12 and under free. Group rates available.

Exhibits include one of three complete sets of Saturday Evening Post covers (324 pieces), over 700 pieces of additional art including the original art for Rockwell's famous War Bond Poster, a replica of his studio, the Four Freedoms Theater which has an eight minute video. Extensive gift shop. Tour should take thirty to forty-five minutes.

THE NORMAN ROCKWELL MUSEUM
Main Street
Stockbridge, MA 01262
413/298-4239

From May through October the museum is open 10 A.M.-5 P.M., Monday-Sunday and November through April, 11 A.M.-4 P.M. Monday-Friday and 10 A.M.-5 P.M. Saturday and Sunday. Guided tours stop at 4:40 P.M. Closed Thanksgiving, Christmas, New Year's Day and last two weeks of January.

Located on Main Street, Stockbridge, Massachusetts.

Reservations requested for groups of ten or more. Admission fee is charged.

This museum contains two floors and shows only original paintings, drawings and sketches by Norman Rockwell which include about fifty paintings on view at any one time. Temporary exhibitions focus on different aspects of Rockwell's Art and the field of illustrations. It offers the public the opportunity to see original art that is so familiar in prints.

THE OFFICIAL
SEBASTIAN MINIATURES MUSEUM
Stacy's Gifts and Collectibles
Route One
Walpole Mall
East Walpole, MA 02032
508/668-4212

Monday-Saturday 9:30 A.M.-9:30 P.M. Sunday 1 P.M.-5 P.M.

Admission in free.

Located in the center of the renovated Stacy's Gifts and Collectibles in the Walpole Mall in East Walpole, Massachusetts. The original museum was dedicated on October 29, 1983 by Sebastian creator Prescott W. Baston.

After a complete store renovation, in 1989 the museum was rededicated by Woody Baston, son of Prescott and now sole sculptor of Sebastian Miniatures.

The museum is comprised of over 1,000 Sebastian Miniatures from the personal collection of the store owners, Sherman and Doris Edwards. It also contains scrapbooks of some early drawings and advertisements that were used as models for many of the original figurines. In the museum are videos that feature the annual Sebastian Festivals and interviews with both Prescott and Woody Baston.

The Official Sebastian Miniatures Museum is located in East Walpole, Massachusetts at Stacy's Gifts & Collectibles. Pictured are owners of Stacy's, Sherman and Doris Edwards, front, along with Woody Baston, son of Prescott and now sole sculptor of Sebastian Miniatures.

UNITED DESIGN PLANT
1600 North Main
Noble, OK 73068
800/727-4883

Plant tours are at 9:30 A.M. and 10:30 A.M., Monday-Friday.

A tour group listens to their tour guide before beginning a tour of United Design's 230,000 square foot manufacturing facility. The tour participants are standing outside the company Gift Shop, where one of every design manufactured is on display and where many are available for purchase by tourists.

Admission is free. Reservations for large groups are requested.

Visitors will see the manufacturing process of United Design figurines. All are produced in Noble, Oklahoma by American artists and craftsmen. The plant is 230,000 square feet and includes the manufacturing, distribution and administration facilities.

The gift shop open during tour hours has one of every design manufactured on display and available for purchase by tourists.

VAILLANCOURT FOLK ART
145 Armsby Rd.
Sutton, MA 01590
508/865-9183

The studio is open Monday-Friday from 9 A.M.-5 P.M., Saturday 11 A.M.-5 P.M. and Sunday 12-5 P.M. Tours are 11 A.M., Monday-Friday.

Admission is free. Reservations are required for groups larger than ten people.

Vaillancourt Folk Art is located in an 1820 New England farmhouse surrounded by stone walls.

The complete tour of the painting studios begins in the moulding room and viewing the antique chocolate moulds. Then the visitors proceed through the painting rooms and then see the finishing process. This shows the creation of the chalkware originals from beginning to end.

Foreign Museums and Tours

THE HOUSE OF ANRI
1-39047 St. Christina
Val Gardena, Italy
617/961-3000 ANRI Headquarters

Tours require advance reservations with Club ANRI to ensure an English-speaking guide. There

Mastercarver Ulrich Bernardi takes a moment to pose with a young man who is touring The House of ANRI in Italy.

is no admission charged. To participate in the tour of the workshop Club membership is required.

Located in Northern Italy near the Austrian border.

Visitors to the workshop will see the artists at work: the step-by-step process of how an ANRI woodcarving is created.

Call for train schedule or car route to the factory.

BELLEEK POTTERY
Belleek Co. Fermanagh
Northern Ireland
Phone 011-44-365-65501 ask for Patricia McCauley

Located in County Fermanagh, Northern Ireland. Free guided tours.

Demonstrations of Belleek's distinctive porcelain weaving and hand assembly. Call before visit to verify when the pottery will be open.

Tours are every half-hour Monday-Friday and the Visitor Center is open Monday-Saturday. The Visitor Center includes a showroom, museum, audio visual room, and restaurant.

The tours provide a chance to see the tradition behind the 133 years of Belleek pottery. On display are all collectible pieces ever made by Belleek and antique pieces dating from 1857. A film of how Belleek pottery is made step-by-step is shown in the audio visual room.

Admission is one British pound, call for American equivalency.

THE ENESCO PRECIOUS MOMENTS COLLECTORS' CLUB TRIP TO THE ORIENT
P.O. Box 1466
Elk Grove Village, IL 60007
Julia Kirkwood
708/640-3195

Tour offered annually every spring. Open to all club members, family and friends.

Precious Moments Collectors' Club members can enjoy a memorable 13-day tour to the Orient. The trip includes stops in Japan, Taiwan, Hong Kong and China. Members tour the Design Studio in Nagoya, Japan, where they will meet the Master Sculptor Yasuhei Fujioka, who personally oversees the original sculpting of each and every Precious Moments figurine. They will also visit the Precious Moments production facilities in Miaoli, Taiwan.

W. GOEBEL PORZELLANFABRIK FACTORY
Postfach 1146/47
W8633 Roedental
From U.S.: 01149-9563920
From Germany: 9536/92303

The factory is located in the county of Coburg, just a few kilometers from the city of the same name.

Factory hours are Monday-Friday, 9 A.M.-12 noon, and Monday-Friday, 1-5:00 P.M.

Visitors will see a film, a special demonstration and be able to shop in the factory store. Members of the M.I. Hummel Club may also be the factory's guest for lunch (but must be there by noon, and advise the receptionist as soon as they arrive); non-members traveling with them pay a nominal amount.

Goebel Factory artist at work.

THE STUDIOS AND WORKSHOPS OF JOHN HINE LIMITED
2 Hillside Road
Aldershot, Hampshire
England GU113NQ
Phone (0252) 334672

The studios and workshops tours are at 10 A.M. and 2 P.M., Monday-Friday.

Admission is free. Reservations are required and can be made by phone or by writing in advance.

Visitors will see the artists' workplaces and demonstrations. On display are new and retired pieces. And visitors are able to browse through the gardens of the restored 16th century barn which houses the studios and workshops.

KAISER PORZELLAN FACTORY TOUR
Alboth & Kaiser GmbH & Co. KG — Postfach 1160
8623 Staffelstein — Germany
Phone (09573) 336-0

Tours can be arranged through Kaiser Porcelain in Niagara Falls (716) 297-2331. No admission charge. Contact Betsy Braun.

Collectors tour the Kaiser factory in Staffelstein, Germany — the heart of Bavarian porcelain making.

KRYSTONIA FACTORY
1 Winpenny Rd.
Chestertow, Staffs., England
Phone (0782) 566636

Tours are by appointment only, Monday-Friday. No admission is charged.

The factory which opened in late 1990 has a guided one-hour tour. Visitors will see the step-by-step process of how a Krystonia figure is produced and decorated. The painters, moldmakers and fettlers will be seen creating the mystical creatures of the Krystonia collection.

Prior to the painting and spraying process, each Krystonia figure is fettled, whereby mold lines are either smoothed or removed.

LLADRO: A COLLECTOR'S ODYSSEY
Lladro Collectors Society
43 West 57th Street
New York, NY 10019-3498

Several tours available for Collector Society members.

Ten day to two week tours of sights in Spain, as well as a tour of the Lladro factory in Valencia. If traveling on own call for appointment to tour factory.

ROMAN HOLIDAY
555 Lawrence Avenue
Roselle, IL 60172
708/529-3000

There will be ten trips in 1992 and the dates will be available in the Spring and Fall of the year. The trips are only available to dealers. For details of trips please call Roman, Inc.

Reservations are required. The cost is tentatively set at $1,992.00 per person (double occupancy).

The trip to Italy will include a full tour of the fascinating process of crafting figurines at the

Fontanini facility in Bagni di Lucca. Travelers will also tour Milan, Ortisei, Florence and many other exciting places.

ROYAL COPENHAGEN PORCELAIN FACTORY
Smallegade 45
2000 Frederikberg, Copenhagen
Denmark
Phone 31 86 48 48

The factory is open from May 15th to September 14th: tours from Monday-Friday, at 9 A.M., 10 A.M., 11 A.M., 1 P.M. and 2 P.M. From September 15th to May 14th: tours from Monday-Friday, at 9 A.M., 10 A.M. and 11 A.M.

Reservations are recommended. For groups of more than five persons, other times for tours can be arranged by prior agreement.

During the tour of the factory, visitors will be told what porcelain is and shown an impressive assortment of porcelain. Visitors will also have the opportunity of seeing porcelain painters at work.

The talk during the one-hour tour is given in Danish, English, German and French.

ROYAL DOULTON FACTORY
Nile Street
Burslem, Stoke-on-Trent
England ST6 2AJ
800/582-2102
Phone (0782) 575454

Admission is free to club members and the non-member admission price is two British pounds per person. Visits for parties of students and senior citizens can be pre-booked at specially reduced rates.

Visitors will see the entire production process

The artisan is modeling the "Old Salt" character jug at The Royal Doulton factory located in Stoke-on-Trent, England.

starting with raw materials to the finished product. The Sir Henry Doulton Gallery is open to visitors which features archives, early wares and the Figures Collection. Tours can be pre-arranged through the Collectors Club or the factory. The tour is completed with a visit to the gift shop and tea room.

ROYAL WORCESTER — DYSON PERRINS MUSEUM
Severn Street
Worcester WR1 2NE
England
Phone (0905) 23221

Open Monday-Friday 9:30 A.M.-5:00 P.M. Saturday 10:00 A.M.-5:00 P.M. Free admission.

Collectors are invited to view the largest collection of Worcester porcelain in the world.

ROYAL WORCESTER FACTORY TOURS
Severn Street
Worcester WR1 2NE
England
Phone (0905) 23221

Factory tours are arranged through the Dyson Perrins Museum. They can be booked in advance by phoning Pam Savage at (0905) 23221.

Two tours are offered:

A standard guided tour of the factory that takes in all stages of the making and decorating processes. Tours last approximately one hour and leave from the Museum at ten minute intervals between 10:25 A.M. and 11:25 A.M. and 1:15 P.M. and 3:15 P.M. Maximum group size twelve. Cost $2.50 (children 8-16 years old $1.50).

The Connoisseurs tour is a more detailed tour for those with more specialized interest. Includes visits to departments not usually open to the general public. Tours last two hours. Two tours a day only — leaving the Museum at 10:15 A.M. and 1:30 P.M. Maximum group size ten (but normally 2 or 4 — very personal!) Cost $7.50 per person includes full color guide book plus morning coffee or afternoon tea.

Note — Safety regulations preclude children less than 8 years old. These tours are also unsuitable for very elderly or disabled persons, due to the number of flights of stairs.

SWAROVSKI CRYSTAL SHOP
A-6112 Wattens
Innstrasse 1
Austria
Phone 05224/5886

May-September, Monday-Saturday, 8 A.M.-6 P.M., Sunday 8 A.M.-12 noon. October-April, Monday-Friday, 8 A.M.-6 P.M., Saturday 8 A.M.-12 noon.

From the Autobahn, take the Wattens exit between Innsbruck and Salzburg/Munich onto Swarovski Strasse.

Visitors can see Swarovski crystal products. Tours highlight artisans cutting, engraving, painting and blowing glass. Gift shop and cafe.

SWAROVSKI COLLECTORS SOCIETY EUROPEAN TOUR
2 Slater Road
Cranston, RI 02920
1-800-426-3088

Tours offered twice a year in the Fall and Spring and limited to members of the Swarovski Collectors Society.

The first part of the tour is spent in Austrian Tyrol, then moves on to the Lake Geneva region of Switzerland. In the Austrian Tyrol, a special visit will be made to Wattens, the home of the Swarovski Company. In Wattens, special exhibits are constructed and members are able to meet Swarovski craftsmen, designers, and technical experts. A private members only shopping experience at the Swarovski Crystal Shop is arranged.

Arrangements are made via an outside travel service.

Information on Other Tours

Factories and museums not listed here may also welcome collectors, even if they do not post specific visiting hours. See addresses in "Company Summaries" to contact any firms that you especially want to visit.